108 Buddhist Parables and Stories

Contents

II   TEACHINGS

III PARABLES

INTRODUCTION

You hold in your hands a collection of the most beloved stories, teachings and parables attributed to Gautama Buddha, the enlightened teacher and sage who lived and taught in the northeastern part of ancient India. His teachings in the form of Jatakas, stories of previous lifetimes, and Sutras, discourses given to monks, composed the foundation of Buddhism and were preserved for approximately twenty-five centuries, mostly through communal recitations held by generations of Buddhist monks and nuns.

These scriptures took their time to reach a modern reader. First Buddhist Sutras written in Pali, Burmese and Sanskrit are thought to be dated to the 1st century BCE, and most of the Jatakas texts are dated to the 3rd-4th century BCE. Only during the second half of the 19th century the first Buddhist texts were translated and introduced into the Western world. The most traditional translation of Jatakas from Pali into English is attributed to E.B. Cowell in his book *The Jataka; or Stories of the Buddha's Former Births* published in 1895; and the translation of Sutras and Jatakas from Burmese to English is attributed to Captain F. Rogers in his work *Buddhaghosha's Parables* published in 1870. Both of these works were used extensively in putting together this book.

Around the same time, a German-American author and philosopher, Paul Carus, compiled ancient Buddhist parables in his masterpiece, *The Gospel of Buddha*, published for the first time in 1894. He discovered stories that exhibit a more mystical tone and describe the Buddha's encounters with demons and celestial devas. Interestingly, some of these stories resemble old Chinese and Indian folk tales, and some even have parallels to early Christian teachings. For one thing, *A Widow's Mite* parable is analogous to *A Lesson of the Widow's Mite* from the Synoptic Gospels (Mark 12:41-44) and is thought to be recorded by Acvaghosha, a Buddhist saint and philosopher who lived in India around 150 CE.

Naturally, this mingling of facts and legends occurred as the narrative of the Buddha's life was retold across cultures, times, and monasteries with many details added along the way. So perhaps, instead of asking how the Buddhist scriptures originated, we should concentrate on what these scriptures do once they enter the world of literature. Quite conceivably, their ability to catalyze deep transformations and find resonance for many people might be the best measure of authenticity. Some Buddhist experts also believe that this multitude of differences and details in Buddhist scriptures reveals a key to understanding them: the diversity of texts is purposeful and immeasurable because of the Buddha's intention to meet the distinctive needs of everyone he anticipated addressing.

From this perspective, the book you are holding is not an exhaustive list of Jatakas and Sutras but a mere scratch on the surface of countless Buddhist scriptures. The idea behind this collection was to include various forms of teachings found in Sutras and concisely present the life story of Gautama Buddha and of his closest disciples. It is my deepest hope that you may find these stories enriching and inspirational. May they bring you a gift of peace, joy and unshakable inner freedom.

I

LIFE OF THE BUDDHA

"One is not a bearer of the teaching by virtue of much speaking, but one who has experienced the truth in person, he is indeed a bearer of the teaching." - Gautama Buddha

One

SIDDHARTHA

Twenty-five centuries ago, in the royal city of Kapilavatthu, King Suddhodana from the great Sakya dynasty ruled a land near the Himalayan Mountains.

His wife, Queen Maya, gave birth to a son in the beautiful flower garden of Lumbini Park. Shortly after the heir's birth, the king was visited by a great sage Asita who had travelled many miles to behold the child. The baby was brought to him, but seeing the child, Asita immediately burst into tears.

Alarmed by this reaction and concerned about its meaning, the king asked Asita to explain why he was saddened. Thus the sage explained, "His future is supreme. Your son shall become an Enlightened One and free the world from its bonds of illusion. I weep only for myself, for I will not live to hear his teachings. For he will give up the kingdom in his indifference to worldly pleasures, and, through bitter struggles grasping the final truth, he will shine forth as a sun of knowledge in the world to dispel the darkness of delusion. With the mighty boat of knowledge, he will bring the world, which is being carried away in affliction, up from the ocean of suffering, which is overspread with the foam of disease and has old age for its waves and death for its fearsome flood."

Though Suddhodana proceeded with a celebration of his son's birth, concern and anxiety began to creep into his mind. The possibility that his son might renounce all that he, the king, held dear in favour of the homeless life and pass his days as a wandering sage - was difficult for Suddhodana to bear. The king called upon eight brahmin priests, all skilled in interpreting astrology signs, and asked them to prophesy for the prince.

When the brahmins had conferred, they said, "According to the signs, your son will certainly become either an enlightened seer or the greatest monarch, a chakravartin, on earth. Should he desire earthly sovereignty, then by his might and law he will stand on earth at the head of all kings. Should he desire salvation and renounce his home and family for the life of a seeker, then by his knowledge and truth, he will overcome all creeds and save the world from its ignorance and folly."

The king asked, "What would cause my son to renounce home and family?"

The brahmins replied, "Seeing the four signs."

"And what are the four?"

"An old man, a sick man, a dead man, and a holy man."

"Then none of these shall he see," the king declared and placed guards around the palace to keep all such persons away.

The king desired his son to inherit the throne and rule in his stead. For Suddhodana, nothing would be better than to see his son become the greatest monarch on earth and to bring the Sakya kingdom to new heights of glory. The king named the boy Siddhartha, meaning 'he who achieved his goals.'

Seven days after giving birth Queen Maya died. The infant prince was nursed and raised by the queen's sister Pajapati, also married to King Suddhodana.

Two

THE SWAN

One day Prince Siddhartha was walking in his father's royal garden with his cousin Devadatta, who had brought his bow and arrows with him. Suddenly, Devadatta saw a swan flying and shot at it. The arrow pierced the swan's body, and the poor creature fell from the sky. Both the boys ran to get the bird. As Siddhartha could run faster than Devadatta, he reached the swan's injured body first and found that it was still alive. He gently pulled out the arrow from the wing. He then got a little juice from cool leaves, put it on the wound to stop the bleeding and stroked the frightened swan. When Devadatta came to claim the swan, Prince Siddhartha refused to give it to him.

"Give me my bird! I shot it down," shouted Devadatta, angry that his cousin was keeping the swan away from him.

"No, I will not give it to you," said the prince. "If you had killed it, it would have been yours. But now, since it is only wounded, it belongs to me."

Devadatta still did not agree, and a strong argument ensued between the two. So both of them decided to go to the king's court, where the counsellors argued the merits of each case. In the end, the king referred the case to his wisest ministers, who, after examining the pros and cons, declared, "A life certainly must belong to the one who tries to save it; a life cannot belong to the one who is only trying to destroy it. The wounded swan by right belongs to Siddhartha."

But Devadatta was still adamant in his claim. So the wise judge made Siddhartha and Devadatta stand at a distance apart from each other and then put the bird in the middle. As the swan started walking towards its saviour, Siddhartha became the rightful owner of the bird.

Three

FIRST MEDITATION

When Siddhartha was nine, King Suddhodana, his royal family and all his ministers attended the ceremony of the first plowing of the fields. On that day Siddhartha saw the actual plowing; he saw a man naked to the waist prodding a water buffalo to pull a plow. It was very close to noon, and the sun shone relentlessly on the man's bareback. He was sweating profusely and visibly tired from walking up and down in the field making the furrows. Intermittently, he would whip the reluctant buffalo. The buffalo had to pull very hard with the yoke upon its body. The plow turned up the soil exposing the worms that made their homes there. Siddhartha then realized why so many small birds were hovering near the ground. They were eating the live worms and other tiny bugs that laid bare for their easy picking. Just then, a hawk swooped down and caught one of the small birds.

Siddhartha watched in silence. He felt the toil of the man who ploughed the field. He felt the struggle of the water buffalo chained to the plow. He felt the pain of the worms cut by the plow. It was heart-wrenching to witness the worms, the insects, and the small bird losing their lives so abruptly.

The noonday sun was scorching. Siddhartha took shelter under a rose-apple tree. After sitting quietly for a while, Siddhartha thought about what he saw and recognized that the man, the water buffalo, the birds, and the worms had one thing in common: each of them was tied to the conditions of its life. A worm was tied to the condition that it was a food source for birds. A small bird was bound by the condition that it might fall prey to larger birds. A water buffalo had to live in captivity and work for its captors.

He recognized that life conditions brought fear and pain at times and enjoyment at others. At one moment, the small bird was enjoying the worms, but in the next moment, it was food for the hawk. Siddhartha observed that the conditions were different for everyone. Some animals enjoyed a greater degree of freedom and safety than others. The peacocks of the royal gardens certainly led a better existence than that of a water buffalo. It was the same with people. One thing stood out above all else: regardless of what conditions they were born with, all living things had a universal wish to live in peace and happiness. All living things wanted to avoid suffering.

King Suddhodana saw Siddhartha sitting under the tree, and in the king's heart, his greatest fear was taking shape: Siddhartha would leave him one day in search of the truth.

Four

THE TIES OF LIFE

As Siddhartha grew to manhood, King Suddhodana sought ways to strengthen the prince's ties to home. The king married him to the lovely Princess Yasodhara, daughter of the king of Koliya. Surrounded by luxury, the prince became a creature of pleasure and seldom left the palace which the king had given to Siddhartha. All sorrowful sights, misery, and knowledge of misery were kept away from Siddhartha, for the king desired no troubles to come near his son. The prince should not know that there was evil in the world.

In the wedlock of Siddhartha and Yasodhara was born a son, whom they named Rahula, meaning 'fetter' or 'tie.' King Suddhodana was glad that an heir was born to his son and said, "The prince having begotten a son will love him as I love the prince. This will be a strong tie to bind Siddhartha's heart to the interests of the world, and the kingdom of the Sakyas will remain under the sceptre of my descendants."

Five

THE THREE WOES

As the chained elephant longs for the wilds of the jungles, so the prince got bored with the royal entertainments and asked his father for permission to see the world outside of the palace. King Suddhodana ordered a jewel-fronted chariot and commanded the roads to be adorned where his son would pass and cleared of the old, sick, dead and holy men. Yet the celestial beings had other plans for Siddhartha.

The houses of the city were decorated with curtains and banners, and spectators arranged themselves on either side, eagerly gazing at the heir to the throne. Thus Siddhartha rode with Channa, his charioteer, through the streets of the city, and into a country watered by rivulets and covered with pleasant trees.

Suddenly, by the wayside an old man appeared with bent frame, wrinkled face and sorrowful brow. The prince asked the charioteer, "Who is this? His head is white, his eyes are bleared, and his body is withered. He can barely walk."

At first the charioteer did not dare to speak the truth. But eventually, much embarrassed, he said, "These are the symptoms of old age. This same man was once a suckling child, and as a youth full of life; but now, as years have passed away, his beauty is gone and the strength of his life is wasted."

Siddhartha was greatly affected by the words of the charioteer, and he sighed because of the pain of old age. 'What joy or pleasure can men take,' he thought to himself, 'when they know they must soon wither and pine away!'

Shortly after they were passing on, a sick man appeared on the way-side gasping for breath. His body was disfigured, convulsed and groaning with pain. The prince asked his charioteer, "What kind of man is this?"

The charioteer replied, "This man is sick. The four elements of his body are out of order. We are all subject to such conditions: the poor and the rich, the ignorant and the wise, all creatures that have bodies are liable to the same calamity."

And Siddhartha was still more moved. All pleasures appeared stale to him, and he loathed the joys of life.

The charioteer sped the horses on to escape the dreary sight, when out of a sudden they were stopped in their course by four persons passing by and carrying a corpse. The prince, shuddering at the sight of a lifeless body, asked the charioteer, "What is this they carry? There are streamers and flower garlands; but the men that follow are overwhelmed with grief!"

The charioteer replied, "This is a dead man. His life is gone; his thoughts are still; his family and friends now carry his corpse to the burnings grounds."

"Is this the only dead man or does the world contain other instances?" asked Siddhartha filled with awe and terror.

With a heavy heart the charioteer replied, "All over the world it is the same.

He who begins life must end it. There is no escape from death."

With bated breath and stammering accents the prince exclaimed, "O worldly men! How fatal is your delusion! Inevitably your body will crumble to dust, yet carelessly you live on."

The charioteer, observing the deep impression these sights had made on the prince, turned his horses and drove back to the city. Siddhartha having returned home looked with disdain upon the treasures of his palace. His wife welcomed him and entreated him to tell her the cause of his grief. He said, "I see everywhere the impression of change; therefore, my heart is heavy. Men grow old, sicken, and die. That is enough to take away the zest of life."

The king, hearing that the prince had become estranged from pleasure, was greatly overcome with sorrow.

Six

RENUNCIATION

The night after his trip to the city, the prince could not fall asleep. Siddhartha went out into the garden, sat down beneath the great jambu tree and gave himself to thought. Pondering on life and death and the evils of decay, he became free from confusion and saw all the misery and sorrow of the world, the pains of pleasure, and the inevitable certainty of death that hovers over every being. A deep compassion seized his heart.

While the prince was concentrating on the problem of evil, he saw a lofty figure endowed with majesty, calm and dignified.

"Who are you?" asked the prince.

The vision responded, "I am a hermit. Troubled at the thought of old age, disease, and death I have left my home to seek the path of salvation. All things hasten to decay; only the truth is forever. Everything changes, and there is no permanency. I long for the happiness that does not decay; the treasure that will never perish; the life that knows of no beginning and no end. Therefore, I have retired to live in solitude and I devoted myself to the search of truth."

Siddhartha asked, "Can peace be gained in this world of unrest? I am struck with the emptiness of pleasure and have become disgusted with lust. All oppresses me, and existence itself seems intolerable."

The hermit replied, "Where heat is, there is also a possibility of cold; creatures subject to pain possess the faculty of pleasure; the origin of evil indicates that good can be developed. For these things are correlatives. Thus where there is much suffering, there will be much bliss. A man who has fallen into a heap of filth ought to seek the great pond of water covered with lotuses. If the lake is not sought, it is not the fault of the lake. Even so when there is a blessed road leading the man held fast by wrong to the liberation, if the road is not walked upon, it is not the fault of the road, but of the person."

A thrill of joy passed through Siddhartha's heart, and he exclaimed, "Now is the time to seek the truth; now is the time to sever all ties that would prevent me from attaining liberation; now is the time to wander into homelessness to find the path of deliverance."

The celestial messenger heard the resolution of Siddhartha with approval. "Now, indeed," he added, "is the time to seek the truth. Go, Siddhartha, and accomplish your purpose. For you are the Buddha; you are destined to enlighten the world. Persevere in your quest for the truth and you shall find what you seek. Pursue your aim diligently, struggle earnestly and you shall conquer." Then the vision vanished.

Siddhartha's heart was filled with peace, and he said, "I have awakened to the truth and I am resolved to accomplish my purpose."

The prince returned to the bedroom of his wife to take a last farewell glance at those whom he dearly loved. There Siddhartha stood gazing at his beautiful wife and his beloved son, and his heart grieved. The pain of parting overcame him powerfully. Although his mind was determined that nothing, be it good or evil, could shake his resolution, the tears flowed from his eyes.

Eventually Siddhartha exited the palace and thus renounced power and worldly pleasures, gave up his kingdom, severed all ties, and went into homelessness. He rode out into the silent night, accompanied only by his faithful charioteer Channa.

Seven

KING BIMBISARA

Shortly after leaving his kingdom, Siddhartha cut his waving hair and exchanged his royal robe for a simple dress. The prince asked his charioteer Channa to bear a message to King Suddhodana that Siddhartha had left the world to walk with a beggar's bowl in his hand.

Still, the majesty of the prince was not well concealed under the poverty of his appearance. His posture exposed his royal birth and his eyes beamed with a fervid zeal for truth. All the people who saw this unusual sight gazed at him in wonder. There was no one who did not pay him homage.

Having entered the city of Rajagraha, the prince went from house to house silently waiting till the people offered him food. Wherever Siddhartha came, people gave him what they had; they bowed before him in humility and were filled with gratitude because he condescended to approach their homes. Old and young people were moved and said, "This is a noble monk! His approach is bliss. What a great joy for us!"

King Bimbisara, noticing the commotion in the city, inquired its cause. When he learned the news, he sent one of his attendants to observe the stranger. Having heard that the monk must be a Sakya and of a noble family and that he had retired to the bank of a flowing river in the woods to eat the food in his bowl, the king was moved in his heart. He donned his royal robe and went out in the company of aged and wise counselors to meet this mysterious guest.

The king found Siddhartha seated under a tree. Contemplating the composure of his face and the gentleness of his deportment, Bimbisara greeted him reverently and said, "O monk, your hands are fit to grasp the reins of an empire and should not hold a beggar's bowl. I am sorry to see you wasting your youth. Believing that you are of royal descent, I invite you to join me in the government of my country and share my royal power. The desire for power and wealth should not be despised by noble-minded. To grow rich and lose religion is not a true gain. But he who possesses all three, power, wealth, and religion, enjoying them in discretion and with wisdom, him I call a great master."

The Blessed One lifted his eyes and replied, "You are known, O King, to be liberal and religious, and your words are prudent. A kind man who makes good use of wealth is rightly said to possess a great treasure, but the miser who hoards up his riches will have no profit. Charity is rich in returns; charity is the greatest wealth, for though it scatters, it brings no repentance.

"I have severed all ties because I seek deliverance. How is it possible for me to return to the world? He who seeks religious truth, which is the highest treasure of all, must leave behind all that can concern him or draw away his attention and must be bent upon that one goal alone. He must free his soul from greed, lust, and desire for power.

"I recognized the illusory nature of wealth and will not take poison as food. Will a fish that has been baited still covet the hook, or an escaped bird love the net? Would a rabbit rescued from the serpent's mouth go back to be devoured? Would a man who has burnt his hand with a torch take up the torch again after he had dropped it to the earth? Would a blind man who has recovered his sight desire to spoil his eyes again?

"The sick man suffering from fever seeks a cooling medicine. Shall we advise him to drink that which will increase the fever? Shall we quench a fire by heaping fuel upon it? Pity me not, O King. Rather pity those who are burdened with the cares of royalty and the worry of great riches. They enjoy them in fear and trembling, for they are constantly threatened with a loss of their possessions, and when they die they cannot take along their gold.

"I have put away my royal inheritance and prefer to be free from the burdens of life. Therefore, try not to entangle me in new relationships and duties nor hinder me from completing the work I have begun. I regret to leave you. But I will go to the sages who can teach me religion. May your country enjoy peace and prosperity, and may wisdom be shed upon your rule like the brightness of the noon-day sun. May your royal power be strong and may righteousness be the scepter in your hand."

The king, clasping his hands with reverence, bowed down before the prince and said, "May you obtain that which you seek, and when you will obtained it, come back and take me as your disciple."

The Blessed One parted from the king in friendship and goodwill.

Eight

URUVELA

Siddhartha continued his search and came to a settlement of five hermits in the jungle of Uruvela. When the prince saw the life of those five men, virtuously keeping in check their senses, subduing their passions, and practising austere self-discipline, he admired their earnestness and joined their company.

With holy zeal and a strong heart, the prince gave himself up to meditative thought and rigorous mortification of the body. Whereas the five sages were severe, the prince was severer still, and they revered him, their junior, as their master.

So Siddhartha continued for six years patiently torturing himself and suppressing worldly desires. He trained his body and exercised his mind in the modes of the most rigorous ascetic life. At last, he ate only one hemp grain each day, seeking to cross the ocean of birth and death and to arrive at the shore of deliverance.

When the prince was on the brink of starvation, Mara, the Evil One, approached him and said, "You are emaciated from fasts, and your death is near. What good is your exertion? Choose to live, and you will be able to do good works."

The prince responded, "O Evil One, for what purpose did you come? Let the flesh waste away if that leads to the mind becoming more tranquil. What is life in this world? Death in battle is better to me than that I should live defeated."

And Mara withdrew.

The prince was shrunken and attenuated, and his body was like a withered branch. The fame of his holiness spread in the surrounding countries, and people came from great distances to see him and receive his blessing.

But the Blessed One still was not satisfied. Seeking true wisdom, he did not find it, and he concluded that mortification would not extinguish desire, nor afford enlightenment in ecstatic contemplation.

Seated beneath a jambu tree, he considered the state of his mind and the fruits of his mortification. His body had become weaker, but his fasts had not advanced him in his search for salvation. Therefore, he saw that it was not the right path and decided to abandon it. He went to bathe in the Neranjara river, but when he strove to leave the water, he could not rise because of his weakness. Then espying the branch of a tree and taking hold of it, he raised himself and left the stream. But while returning to his abode, he staggered and fell to the ground, and the five hermits thought he was dead.

There was a chief herdsman living near the grove whose eldest daughter was called Nanda, and Nanda happened to pass by the spot where the Blessed One had swooned. Bowing down before him she offered him rice-milk and the Blessed One accepted the gift. When he had partaken of the rice-milk all his limbs were refreshed, his mind became clear again.

After this happened, the Blessed One again took some food. His disciples, having witnessed this scene and observing the change in their master's mode of living, became filled with suspicion. They were convinced that Siddhartha's religious zeal was flagging and that he had become oblivious of his high purpose.

When the Blessed One saw the hermits turning away from him, he felt sorry for their lack of confidence. Suppressing his grief, he wandered on alone.

Nine

MARA

Siddhartha directed his steps to that Bodhi tree beneath whose shade he was to accomplish his search. When he sat down, the heavens resounded with joy, and all living beings were filled with good cheer. Mara alone, lord of the five desires, bringer of death and enemy of truth, was grieved and rejoiced not. With his three daughters, Tanha, Raga and Arati, the tempters, and with his host of evil demons, he went to where the prince sat.

But Siddhartha heeded him not. Mara uttered fear-inspiring threats and raised a whirlwind so that the skies were darkened and the ocean roared and trembled. The prince under the Bodhi tree remained calm and feared not. Siddhartha knew that no harm could befall him.

The three daughters of Mara tempted the prince, but he paid no attention to them. When Mara saw that he could not inflate any desire in the heart of the victorious monk, he ordered all the evil spirits at his command to attack him. Again Siddhartha watched them as one would watch the harmless games of children. All the fierce hatred of the evil spirits was of no avail. The flames of hell became wholesome breezes of perfume, and the angry thunderbolts were changed into lotus blossoms.

When Mara saw this, he fled away with his army from the Bodhi tree.

Ten

ENLIGHTENMENT

Siddhartha, having put Mara to flight, gave himself up to meditation. All the miseries of the world, the evils produced by evil deeds and the sufferings arising therefrom, passed before his eye, and he uttered, "Surely if living creatures saw the results of all their evil deeds, they would turn away from them in disgust. But selfhood blinds them, and they cling to their desires. They crave pleasure for themselves and they cause pain to others; when death destroys their individuality, they find no peace; their thirst for existence abides and their selfhood reappears in new births. Thus they continue to move in the coil and can find no escape from the hell of their own making. And how empty are their pleasures, how vain are their endeavors! Men go astray because they think that delusion is better than truth."

And he began to expound the Dharma, the universal law of nature. Pondering the origin of birth and death, the prince recognized that ignorance was the root of all evil; and there are the links in the development of life called the twelve nidanas: In the beginning there is existence blind and without knowledge; and in this sea of ignorance there are stirrings formative and organizing. From stirrings, formative and organizing, rises awareness or feelings. Feelings beget organisms that live as individual beings. These organisms develop the six fields: the five senses and the mind. The six fields come in contact with things. Contact begets sensation. Sensation creates the thirst of an individualized being. The thirst of being creates a cleaving to things. The cleaving produces the growth and continuation of selfhood. Selfhood continues in renewed birth. The renewed births of selfhood are the causes of sufferings, old age, sickness, and death. They produce lamentation, anxiety, and despair. If ignorance is removed, then all suffering disappears.

Then Siddhartha saw the four noble truths which pointed out the path to liberation and uttered this verse:

Through many births I sought in vain
The Builder of this House of Pain.
Now, Builder, You are plain to see,
And from this House at last I'm free;
I burst the rafters, roof and wall,
And dwell in the Peace beyond them all.

Blessed is he who understood the Dharma. Blessed is he who does no harm to his fellow-beings and conquered all selfishness and vanity.

Thus Siddhartha has become the Buddha, the Enlightened One, the Blessed One, and he uttered, "I have recognized the deepest truth, which is sublime and peace-giving, but difficult to understand for most men because they move in a sphere of worldly interests and find their delight in worldly desires. There is self and there is truth. Where self is, truth is not. Where truth is, self is not. The attainment of truth is possible only when self is recognized as an illusion. Righteousness can be practiced only when the mind is freed from passions. Perfect peace can dwell only where all vanity has disappeared. The task is impossible for those who only search for happiness in selfhood. The bliss lies in complete surrender to truth. The truth remains hidden from those blinded by craving and aversion. Liberation remains incomprehensible and mysterious to the vulgar minds clouded with worldly interests. Should I preach the doctrine of Dharma and mankind not comprehend it, it would bring me trouble."

On hearing these words of the Blessed One, Mara approached and said, "Be greeted, the Enlightened One. You have attained the highest bliss, and it is time for you to enter the final liberation stage."

Suddenly, Brahma Sahampati descended from the heavens and said, "Alas! The world must perish should the Blessed One decide not to teach the Dharma. Be merciful to those who struggle; have compassion upon the sufferers; pity the creatures who are hopelessly entangled in the snares of sorrow. There are some beings that are almost free from the dust of worldliness. They will be lost if they do not hear the doctrine preached."

The Blessed One, full of compassion, looked upon all sentient creatures with his spiritual eye and saw among them beings whose minds were but scarcely covered by the dust of worldliness. He saw some beings conscious of the dangers of lust and wrong doing and replied to Brahma Sahampati, "Wide open be the door of immortality to all who have ears to hear. May they receive the Dharma."

Then the Buddha turned to Mara and said, "I shall not pass into the final stage of liberation, O Evil One, until the knowledge of truth becomes successful, prosperous, widespread, and popular among men!"

At that moment, Brahma Sahampati understood that the Blessed One had granted his request to preach the doctrine.

Eleven

FIRST CONVERTS

The Blessed One stayed in solitude for seven days, enjoying the bliss of liberation.

At that time Tapussa and Bhallika, two merchants, came traveling on the road nearby. When they saw the great monk, majestic and full of peace, they approached respectfully and offered him rice cakes and honey. This was the first food that the Blessed One ate after becoming the Buddha.

And the Buddha addressed them and explained to them the path of liberation. The two merchants bowed down in reverence and said, "We take our refuge, O Master, in the Blessed One and in the Dharma."

Tapussa and Bhallika became the Buddha's first followers and were lay disciples.

Then Buddha had decided to go to Uruvela and pay homage to the hermits, his former teachers, for sharing their knowledge. But these ascetics were jealous of the Buddha's enlightenment and had conspired to ignore his presence when he arrived. And even though they decided not to welcome him, when the Buddha approached, they all stood up and fell to his feet. His persona was such that it just brought it out in them.

Twelve

THE KING'S GIFT

King Bimbisara having taken his refuge in the Buddha invited the Blessed One with his monks to his palace for a meal.

The Blessed One having donned his robes took his alms bowl and, together with a great number of disciples, entered the city of Rajagraha. Sakka, the king of the devas, assuming the appearance of a young brahmin, walked in front of them, saying, "He who teaches self-control with those who have learned self-control; the redeemer with those whom he has redeemed; the Blessed One with those to whom he has given peace, is entering Rajagraha! Hail to the Buddha! Honor to his name and blessings to all who take refuge in him."

Sakka also intoned this verse:
  Blessed is the place in which the Buddha walks,
  And blessed the ears which hear his talks;
  Blessed his disciples, for they are
  The tellers of his truth both near and far.
  If all could hear this truth so good
  Then all men's minds would eat rich food,

And strong would grow men's brotherhood.

When the Blessed One had finished his meal, the king sat down near him and thought, 'Where may I find a place for the Blessed One to live in, not too far from the town and not too near, suitable for going and coming, easily accessible to all people who want to see him, a place that is by day not too crowded and by night not exposed to noise, wholesome and well fitted for retired life? There is my garden, the bamboo grove Veluvana, fulfilling all these conditions. I shall offer it to the order of monks led by the Buddha.'

Thus the king dedicated his garden to the Sangha, to the order of monks.

Thirteen

RETURN

After nearly seven years of having heard nothing of his son, Suddhodana came to know that Siddhartha was staying at Rajagraha, and that he was claiming to be enlightened. Overjoyed to know that his son was still alive, Suddhodana sent a messenger to ask the prince to return home.

The messenger met the Buddha at Veluvana, the bamboo grove near Rajagraha. But on hearing the words of Dharma there and then, the messenger decided to become a monk, completely forgetting to pass on Suddhodana's message. More messengers were sent, but the same thing happened.

Finally, in exasperation, Suddhodana commissioned his close adviser to take the message but only permitted him to become a monk on the condition that he passed the message to the Buddha.

And so the Buddha came to know of his father's desire to see him. The Blessed One consented to his father's request and set out on his journey to Kapilavatthu. Soon the news spread in the native country of the Buddha that Prince Siddhartha, the one who wandered from home into homelessness to

32

obtain enlightenment, was coming back.

Shortly after, the Buddha came to Kapilavatthu, accompanied by many monks. Upon arrival, they stayed outside the town in a park and entered the town to beg for alms in the morning. Only then Suddhodana learned that the Buddha had arrived and was shocked that his son would sleep under a tree rather than in the palace and beg in the streets rather than feast at the banquet table.

Suddhodana went out with his relatives and ministers to meet the prince. When the king saw Siddhartha, he was struck by his son's beauty and dignity but, unable to contain his anger, uttered, "You are degrading your family's dignity."

The Buddha replied, "You are speaking to your son, the prince, the person who no longer exists. O Suddhodana, on becoming enlightened one becomes a member of the family of the noble ones, and their dignity depends only on wisdom and compassion."

The king realized that the noble monk, his son, was no longer Siddhartha - he was the Buddha, the Blessed One, the Enlightened One, and the Teacher of mankind.

Then the Buddha took a seat opposite his father, and the king gazed eagerly at his son. He longed to call him by his name, but he dared not. "Siddhartha," he exclaimed silently in his heart, "Siddhartha, come back to your aged father and be his son again!" But seeing the determination of his son, he suppressed his sentiments. Sadness overcame him.

"I would offer you my kingdom," the king said, "but if I did, you would treat it as mere ashes."

And the Buddha replied, "I know that the king's heart is full of love and that he feels deep grief for his son's sake. But let go of the ties of love that bind him to the son whom he lost and embrace with equal kindness all his fellow-beings, and he will receive in his place a greater one than Siddhartha; he will receive the Buddha, and the truth will enter into his heart."

Suddhodana trembled with joy when he heard the words of his son, the Buddha, and exclaimed with tears in his eyes, "Alas! The overwhelming sorrow has passed away. At first my heart was heavy, but now I reap the fruit of your great renunciation."

Fourteen

YASODHARA, THE FORMER WIFE

When the Suddhodana conducted the Buddha into the palace, all the ministers and the royal family members greeted him with great reverence. Yet, Yasodhara, the prince's wife, did not make her appearance. The king sent for Yasodhara, but she replied, "Surely, if I am deserving of any regard, Siddhartha himself will come and see me."

Having greeted all his relatives and friends, the Blessed One asked, "Where is Yasodhara?" And on being informed that she had refused to come, he rose straightway and went to her apartments.

"I am free," the Blessed One said to his disciples, Sariputta and Moggallana, whom he had asked to accompany him to the princess' chamber. "But the princess, however, is not yet free. Not having seen me for a long time, she is exceedingly sorrowful. Unless her grief is to be allowed its course, her heart will cleave."

Yasodhara sat in her room, dressed in simple garments and with her hair cut. When Prince Siddhartha entered, she was, from the abundance of her affection, like an overflowing vessel, unable to contain her love. Forgetting

35

that the man she loved was the Buddha, she held him by his feet and wept bitterly.

Remembering, however, that King Suddhodana was present, she felt ashamed and seated herself reverently at a little distance.

The king apologized for the princess, saying, "This arises from her deep affection and is not a temporary emotion. During the seven years that she had lost her husband when she heard that Siddhartha had shaved his head, she did likewise; when she heard that he had left off the use of perfumes and ornaments, she also refused their use. Like her husband she had eaten at appointed times from an earthen bowl only. Like him she had renounced high beds with splendid coverings, and when other princes asked her in marriage, she replied that she was still his. Therefore, grant her forgiveness."

And the Blessed One spoke kindly to Yasodhara, telling of her great merits inherited from former lives. She had indeed been again and again of great assistance to him. Her purity, her gentleness, her devotion had been invaluable to the Blessed One when he aspired to attain enlightenment. And so holy had she been that she desired to become the wife of a Buddha. This karma was a result of great merits.

Later, Yasodhara took a threefold refuge and, ordained as a nun, became one of the first women to enter the Sangha.

Fifteen

RAHULA, THE SON

When the Buddha returned to Kapilavatthu, Yasodhara took little Rahula to listen to the Buddha's preaching. When they arrived, she said to her son, "This is your father, Rahula. Go and ask him for your inheritance." The child walked through the assembly and stood before the Buddha, saying without fear and with much affection, "How pleasant is your shadow, O Monk." When the talk had finished and the Buddha left, Rahula followed him, and as they walked along Rahula said, "Give me my inheritance, O Monk."

The Buddha had nothing to give except the doctrine of Dharma, so he turned to Sariputta and said, "My son asks for his inheritance. I cannot give him perishable treasures that will bring cares and sorrow, but I can give him the inheritance of a holy life, a treasure that will not perish. "

When King Suddhodana heard that Rahula had joined the brotherhood of monks, he was grieved. He had lost his son, Siddhartha, and now he had lost his only grandson. And the Blessed One promised that from that time forward he would not ordain any minor without the consent of his parents or guardians.

As if to make up for the seven years the boy was without a father, the Buddha took great interest in Rahula's moral and spiritual education, teaching him many times himself. Rahula was an eager and attentive student, and it is said that each morning as he awoke, he would take a handful of sand and say, "May I have today as many words of counsel from my teacher as there are here grains of sand." As a result of this enthusiasm, the Buddha said that of all his disciples Rahula had the most zeal for training.

The conduct of Rahula, however, was not always marked by a love of truth, and so the Blessed One ordered his son to bring him a basin of water and to wash his feet, to which Rahula obeyed.

When Rahula had washed his father's feet, the Blessed One asked him, "Is the water now fit for drinking?"

"No, Master," replied Rahula, "the water is unclean."

Said the Blessed One, "Now consider your own case, Rahula. You are unable to guard your tongue from untruth, and thus your mind is unclean."

And when the water had been poured away, the Buddha asked again, "Is this vessel now fit for holding water to drink?"

"No, Master," replied Rahula, "the vessel, too, has become unclean."

"Now consider your own case, Rahula. Are you fit for any high purpose when you have become unclean like the vessel?"

Then the Blessed One lifting up the empty basin and whirling it round said to Rahula, "Are you not afraid that it might fall and break?"

"No, Master, it is cheap; its loss will not amount to much," replied Rahula,

"Now consider your own case, Rahula. Your mind is whirled about in endless thoughts, and your body is made of the same substance as other material things that will crumble to dust. There is no loss if it to be broken."

The Buddha then impressed upon his son the importance of speaking the truth, saying, "Rahula, for anyone who has no shame at intentional lying, there is no evil that that person cannot do. Therefore, you should train yourself never to tell a lie." Having explained what has to be done, the Buddha went on to explain to Rahula how it could be done.

"Rahula, what is the purpose of a mirror?"

"The purpose of a mirror is to look at yourself."

"Just so, Rahula, one should act with body, speech or mind only after first looking at oneself. Before acting with body, speech or mind, one should think, 'What I am about to do, will it harm me or others?' If you can answer, 'Yes, it will,' then you should not act. But if you can answer, 'No, it will not,' then you should act. You should reflect in the same way while acting and after having acted. Therefore, Rahula, you should train yourself to act only after repeatedly looking at and reflecting on yourself."

Rahula was trained in monastic discipline, and when he was eighteen, the Buddha decided that he was ready for meditation. The Blessed One then gave Rahula advice on how to practice, saying, "Develop a mind that is like the four great elements (earth, water, fire and air) because if you do this, pleasant or unpleasant sensory impressions that have arisen and taken hold of the mind will not persist. Develop love, Rahula, for by doing so you will get rid of ill-will. Develop compassion, for by doing so you will get rid of violence. Develop sympathetic joy, for by doing so you will get rid of animosity. Develop equanimity, for by doing so you will get rid of uncontrolled reaction. Develop the perception of the foul, for by doing so you will get rid of attachment. Develop the perception of impermanence, for by doing so you will get rid of the conceit of selfhood. Develop mindfulness of breathing for it is of great benefit and advantage."

Following his father's advice and guidance on meditation, Rahula finally attained enlightenment. After that everyone always referred to him as Rahulabhadda meaning 'Rahula the Lucky'.

Sixteen

THE PEACEMAKER

Once when the Buddha was staying at the Nyagrodha Park near Kapilavatthu, a serious dispute broke out between the Sakyas and Koliyas, who had directed the Rohini river to be constricted by a dam between the cities of Kapilavatthu and Devadaha for irrigation of their fields.

In a certain month, when the crops started to wither and the river ran low, labourers and residents of both the cities assembled for a meeting. The Koliyas remarked that if the water continued to be shared by both sides, it would be inadequate for both clans. And since their crops could ripen with one more watering, they should have it. To that, the Sakyas rebutted that their crops, too, could ripen with one more watering, and they should have the water.

Thus began their bickering out of mutual reluctance to let the water be taken by the other. When things got more bitter, one man struck another, with the other man retaliating and sparking off a fight. Both sides reported the quarrel to their ministers, who, in turn, reported it to their royal households. And the leaders of the respective clans also got infuriated and decided to wage war on each other. Armed for battle, the Sakyas and Koliyas declared

41

to show their strength and power to each other.

Surveying the world at dawn, the Buddha realized that they would destroy one another if he did not go to them. Using his supernormal power, he levitated through the air to where the conflict was and sat cross-legged above the middle of the Rohini river to catch everyone's attention.

The Sakyas and Koliyas, on seeing this amazing miracle, threw off their weapons and paid homage to the Blessed One.

Then the Buddha enquired about the origin of the quarrel and got a response that the quarrel began over not sharing the water.

The Blessed One asked the kings, "Tell me, O Kings, how much the water is worth?"

"Very little, of course," responded the kings.

"And how much the human lives are worth?"

"Beyond the price," replied the kings.

"Is it fitting, O Kings, that for very little water one should destroy human lives which are beyond price?"

And to this, all became silent. The Buddha then asked both sides to reflect on their actions, exclaiming that if he were not there, they would have let a river of blood flow out of their evil desires.

Seventeen

ANANDA

Many people in Kapilavatthu listened to the Buddha's teachings and took refuge in his doctrine, among them Nanda, Siddhartha's half-brother; Devadatta, his cousin; Upali the barber; and Anuruddha the philosopher. Some years later, Ananda, another cousin of the Blessed One, also joined the Sangha.

The Buddha was always accompanied by an attendant whose job was to run messages for him, prepare his seat, and attend to his personal needs. For the first twenty years of his ministry, he had several attendants, Nagasamala, Upavana, Nagita, Cunda, Radha, and others, but none proved suitable. One day, when he decided to replace his present attendant, he called all the monks and addressed them, "I am now getting old and wish to have someone as a permanent attendant. Which of you would like to be my attendant?"

All the monks enthusiastically offered their services, except Ananda, who modestly sat at the back in silence. Later, when asked why he had not volunteered he replied that the Buddha knew best who to pick. When the Buddha indicated that he would like Ananda to be his personal attendant, Ananda said he would accept the position, but only on eight conditions.

The first four conditions were that the Buddha should never give him any of the food nor any of the robes, that the Blessed One received, that he should not be given any special accommodation, and that he would not have to accompany the Buddha when the Blessed One accepted invitations to people's homes. Ananda insisted on these four conditions because he did not want people to think that he was serving the Buddha out of desire for a material gain.

The last four conditions were related to Ananda's desire to help in the promotion of the Dharma. These conditions were: that if Ananda was invited to a meal, he could transfer the invitation to the Buddha; that if people came from outlying areas to see the Buddha, Ananda would have the privilege of introducing them; that if he had any doubts about the Dharma, he should be able to talk to the Buddha about them at any time and that if the Buddha gave a discourse in his absence, the Blessed One would later repeat it in his presence. The Buddha smilingly accepted these conditions.

Ananda was a man after the heart of the Blessed One; he was his most beloved disciple, profound in comprehension and gentle in spirit. He remained always near the Buddha until the death parted them.

Eighteen

SARIPUTTA AND MOGGALLANA

Sariputta and Moggallana, two brahmin priests, led a very religious life. They had promised each other that the one who first attains enlightenment shall tell the other one.

Once Sariputta saw monk Assaji who was dignified in manners and was begging for alms modestly keeping his eyes to the ground. Sariputta exclaimed, "Truly, this monk has entered the right path; I will ask him in whose name he has retired from the world and what doctrine he professes."

Being addressed by Sariputta, Assaji replied, "I am a follower of the Buddha, the Blessed One, but being a novice I can tell you the substance only of the doctrine."

Sariputta exclaimed, "Tell me! It is the substance I want."

Then Assaji recited this stanza:
Nothing we seek to touch or see
Can represent Eternity.
They spoil and die: then let us find

Eternal Truth within the mind.

Having heard this stanza, Sariputta said, "Now I see clearly, whatsoever is subject to origination is also subject to cessation. If this is the doctrine, I have reached the state to enter the path of liberation which before has remained hidden from me."

Then Sariputta went to Moggallana and told him about the Buddha's teachings, and both decided to go to the Blessed One.

When the Buddha saw Sariputta and Moggallana coming from afar, he said to his disciples, "These two monks are highly auspicious." The two friends had taken refuge in the Buddha, the Dharma and the Sangha and became loyal and virtuous disciples.

Nineteen

KASSAPA

As soon as the number of disciples reached sixty, the Buddha sent them away to teach people in other regions. He left the Deer Park and turned southwards towards the Magadha country.

Along the way, on the banks of a river lived three brothers whose names were Uruvela Kassapa, Nadi Kassapa and Gaya Kassapa. Each lived with 500, 300 and 200 followers, respectively. These were brahmin hermits with matted hair, worshiping the fire and keeping a fire-dragon. They were renowned throughout India, and their names were honored as some of the wisest men.

The Blessed One paid a visit to Uruvela Kassapa and said, "Let me stay a night in the room where you keep your sacred fire."

Seeing the Blessed One in his majesty and beauty, Kassapa thought, 'This is a great monk and a noble teacher. Should he stay overnight in the room where the sacred fire is kept, the fire-dragon will bite him, and he will die.' Kassapa then warned the Buddha, saying, "I do not object to you staying overnight in the room where the sacred fire is kept, but the dragon lives there; he will harm you."

Still, the Buddha insisted, and Kassapa admitted him to the room where the sacred fire was kept. And the Blessed One sat down with body erect, surrounding himself with mindfulness. In the night the dragon came, belching forth in rage his fiery poison, and filling the air with burning vapor, but could do the Buddha no harm. The fire consumed itself while the Blessed One remained composed. In the end, the venomous serpent became so wroth that he died in his anger.

In the morning, the Blessed One showed the dragon's dead body to Kassapa and said, "His fire has been conquered by my fire." And Kassapa thought, 'He is a great monk and possesses high powers, but he is not holy like me.'

There was in those days a festival, and Kassapa thought, 'The people will come from all parts of the country and see the great Buddha. When he speaks to them, they will believe him and abandon me.' And he grew envious. When the day of the festival arrived, the Blessed One retired and did not come to Kassapa.

Kassapa went to the Buddha the following day and said, "Why did you not come?"

The Buddha replied, "Did not you think, Kassapa, that it would be better if I stayed away from the festival?"

Kassapa was astonished and thought, 'Great is this monk; he can read my most secret thoughts, but he is not holy like me.'

Then the Blessed One addressed Kassapa, saying, "You see the truth, but do not accept it because of the envy that dwells in your heart. Is this envy wholesome? Envy is the last remnant of self that has remained in your mind."

And Kassapa gave up his resistance. His envy disappeared, and, bowing down, he said, "O Master, let me receive the ordination from the Blessed

One." Then Kassapa went to his followers and said, "I am anxious to lead a religious life under the direction of the great Buddha, who is the Enlightened One. Do what you think is best."

Kassapa's followers replied, "We have conceived a profound affection for the great Buddha, and if you are joining his Sangha, we will do likewise." And all of them took refuge in the Buddha, the Dharma, and the Sangha. This is how the following of the Blessed One grew by another thousand devotees.

Twenty

ANATHAPINDIKA, THE MAN OF WEALTH

One of the Buddha's most devout followers was a wealthy merchant named Sudatta. He was famous for his donations to the hungry and homeless and became known as Anathapindika meaning 'friend of the poor.'

Anathapindika lived in Sravastti. One day he traveled to Rajagraha to visit his brother-in-law. The household was so busy preparing for a feast that Anathapindika failed to get his usual warm welcome.

"What is the big occasion?" Anathapindika asked his brother-in-law, "Are you preparing for a great wedding or perhaps a visit from the king?"

"No," his brother-in-law responded. "The Buddha and his monks are coming for a meal tomorrow."

Just hearing the word 'Buddha' filled Anathapindika with such joy that he could hardly contain himself and said, "You mean that a fully enlightened being has arisen in the world? How wonderful! Take me to meet him".

Anathapindika wanted to go straight away, but he was persuaded that it was too late and that it would be better to do so the next morning. That night Anathapindika was so excited that he could hardly sleep. Eventually Anathapindika set off to meet the Buddha thinking that the sun would be rising soon. But as he entered the city's outskirts and it was still dark, he became frightened and decided to turn back. Suddenly, a friendly spirit appeared illuminating the whole area and urged him to continue, saying, "Walk on! To move forward is better for you than to turn back."

Encouraged by these words, Anathapindika continued and soon came across the Buddha walking up and down in the early morning light. The Buddha saw Anathapindika hesitating to come closer, so the Blessed One beckoned him and said, "Come forward, Sudatta."

Astonished that the Buddha would know his real name and awed by the great man's presence, Anathapindika hurried forward and bowed at the Buddha's feet. The two men talked together for some time, and as the sun came up, Anathapindika understood the essence of the Dharma.

Anathapindika then asked the Buddha if he could offer him a meal the next day, and the Buddha accepted. During the day Anathapindika thought about how wonderful it would be if the Buddha could come to Sravastti and how many people would benefit from this visit. Consequently, the next day, after the Buddha had finished his meal, Anathapindika asked him if he would come and visit Sravastti. The Buddha agreed, adding, "Enlightened ones prefer to stay in peaceful places." Anathapindika responded, "I fully understand, Master."

When Anathapindika finished his business in Rajagraha, he set out for Sravastti. And as soon as he arrived, he began to make preparations for the Buddha's arrival. To start, he had to find a suitable place for the Buddha and his monks to stay, near the city but not too noisy. The best place proved to be a park about one-kilometre southwest of the walls of Sravastti, owned by Prince Jeta. Anathapindika approached the prince and asked him if he wanted to sell his park. The prince declined. Anathapindika insisted, but Prince Jeta reiterated that he was not interested in selling.

"I will pay you any price you choose," Anathapindika said.

To put the merchant off, the prince answered, "All right! You can have the park for however much it costs to cover the ground with gold coins."

To the prince's astonishment, Anathapindika enthusiastically agreed and left straight away to get the money. Soon a wagon full of gold arrived at the park, and servants began spreading the money on the ground. When Prince Jeta saw this, he realized how determined Anathapindika was to get the park and finally decided to accept a more reasonable price for it.

Then Anathapindika built living quarters, assembly halls, storerooms and pavilions, laid out gardens and dug ponds. At the same time, Prince Jeta offered to build an impressive gatehouse leading into the park and a wall around it for privacy. In recognition of the two men who made all this possible, the monastery was named Jeta's Grove, Anathapindika's Park or just Jetavana for short.

From the age of sixty, the Buddha spent every rainy season except his last at Jeta's Grove and delivered more discourses there than at any other location. The Buddha's favourite places in Jetavana were two small houses: the Kosambakuti and the Gandhakuti meaning 'fragrant hut'. Gandhakuti got its name because of the flowers that people constantly brought to offer to the Buddha.

Although Anathapindika built the Jetavana, this was certainly not the extent of his generosity. Over the years, he spent vast amounts of money providing the five requisites for monks, building and maintaining monasteries, and doing charity in the name of Buddhism. He understood that if wealth is used with generosity and compassion, it could be an excellent tool for spiritual development. Throughout its history, Buddhism has been assisted in its establishment and spread by the generous support from wealthy merchants and businessmen, but the first and greatest was Anathapindika.

Twenty-One

PROTECTING THE BUDDHA

On a certain occasion, Anathapindika entertained the Buddha in his house. Anathapindika wanted his guest to give a teaching, but concerned the Blessed One might be weary and tired, he refrained from asking. But as soon as Anathapindika took his seat, the Buddha read his thoughts and said, "You protect me where I have no need to be protected. For I spent four periods of time of incalculable length, and a hundred thousand cycles of time in addition, acquiring and perfecting the knowledge. And all this I did so that I might teach others." And straightɸway the Buddha gave a teaching of Dharma to Anathapindika.

Twenty-Two

THE JEALOUSY OF DEVADATTA

Ever since he was young, Devadatta had been jealous of Siddhartha. When the Blessed One achieved enlightenment and returned with a visit to Kapilavatthu, Devadatta decided to become a disciple counting to attain the same distinctions and honors as Siddhartha. He resented constantly being in the Buddha's shadow and hoped that if the Buddha died or got too old, Devadatta had a good chance to take over the leadership of the Sangha. Despite his unpleasant nature Devadatta was not without talent; he had developed psychic powers, which had attracted many admirers. Unfortunately, his powers and the attention he received only made him more proud and ambitious.

One day, as the Buddha sat with a large company of monks, Devadatta came forward, bowed and said, "O Master, leading the Sangha at your age must be a great burden. Step down and I will lead the Sangha for you. I will take over this responsibility so that you can live in comfort." Devadatta thought that the other monks, being concerned for the Buddha's welfare, would be delighted with this idea and urge the Buddha to retire. The Buddha was, however, well aware of Devadatta's intentions and firmly turned down this idea. Devadatta was humiliated by this rebuke, and within his heart he vowed to revenge.

Twenty-Three

AJATASATTU AND DEVADATTA

After Devadatta got disappointed in his ambitions to replace the Buddha as a leader of the Sangha, he conceived in his heart even more hatred. Attempting to excel the Buddha in virtue, Devadatta found fault with the regulations of the Sangha and reproved them as too lenient.

At about this time Prince Ajatasattu was becoming increasingly impatient to ascend to the throne. His father, King Bimbasara, had ruled for many years, and it looked likely that he would continue to rule for many more, which meant that Ajatasattu himself would be old before he himself became king. Devadatta knew of Prince Ajatasattu's predicament and, seeing that he had something in common with him, decided that they should work together. He used his psychic powers to impress the prince.

From that time, Devadatta had free access to the royal palace, and Prince Ajatasattu often waited upon him with lavish food and expensive gifts. Ajatasattu built a new monastery for Devadatta and founded an order that prescribed severe rules and self-mortification to disciples.

Soon afterwards, the Blessed One himself came to Rajagraha and stayed at this monastery. Devadatta called on the Blessed One requesting him to sanction his rules of greater stringency, and said, "The body consists of its thirty-two parts and has no divine attributes. It is conceived in sin and born in corruption. Its attributes are a liability to pain and dissolution, for it is impermanent. It is the receptacle of karma which is the curse of our former existences; it is the dwelling place of diseases and its organs constantly discharge disgusting secretions. Its end is death and its goal is the charnel house. Therefore, we have to treat the body as a carcass full of abomination and to clothe it in rags only."

The Buddha replied, "Truly, the body is full of impurity and its end is the charnel house, for it is impermanent and destined to be dissolved into its elements. But being the receptacle of karma, it lies in our power to make it a vessel of truth and not evil. It is not good to indulge in the pleasures of the body, but neither is it good to neglect our bodily needs and to heap filth upon impurities.

"The lamp that is not cleansed and not filled with oil will be extinguished, and a body that is unkempt, unwashed, and weakened by penance will not be a fit receptacle for the light of truth. Attend to your body and its needs as you would treat a wound which you care for. Severe rules will not lead the disciples on the middle path which I have taught. Certainly, no one can be prevented from keeping more stringent rules if he sees fit to do so, but they should not be imposed upon anyone."

Thus the Blessed One refused Devadatta's proposal. Devadatta left the Buddha and went into the monastery speaking evil of the Master's path as too lenient and altogether insufficient. When the Blessed One heard of Devadatta's intrigues, he said, "Among men there is no one who is not blamed. People blame the one who sits silent and the one who speaks; they also blame the man who preaches the middle path."

Twenty-Four

ASSASSINATION PLAN

One day, after Prince Ajatasattu had complained about his role as a prince, Devadatta persuaded him to kill King Bimbasara to make Ajatasattu the king. In his turn, Devadatta shared his plans to kill the Buddha and make himself the leader of the Sangha. At first Ajatasattu was shocked by this suggestion, but so strong was his ambition and desire for power that he agreed.

So Devadatta instigated Ajatasattu to plot against the Buddha. Ajatasattu listened to the bad advice of Devadatta and gave orders to take the life of the Blessed One. They sent a man to assassinate the Buddha and arranged to have the assassin murdered afterwards so that there would be no witness. The assassin, however, had scruples and hesitated to kill such a holy person. When the man actually stood in front of the Buddha, he broke down and confessed to the Blessed One what he had planned to do. The Buddha forgave him, and the assassin asked to become a Buddha's disciple. When Devadatta heard this, he became furious.

Meanwhile, Ajatasattu strapped a dagger to his thigh and tried to enter the king's bed-chamber. But the guards caught him, and the plot failed. King Bimbasara came to hear of his son's attempts to kill him. Deeply saddened, he decided to step down in his favour. Although no longer king, Bimbasara still supported the Buddha. This worried Devadatta, so he convinced Ajatasattu to kill his father. Ajatasattu ordered Bimbasara to be imprisoned and deprived of food. Queen Kosaladevi, Bimbisara's wife, who was the only person allowed to visit the prisoner, smuggled food concealed in her clothes to the former king. When, after two weeks, Bimbasara was still not dead, Ajatasattu sent men into the prison cell to kill his father. So he ended the life of a just and popular king who was also one of the Buddha's most enthusiastic supporters.

Twenty-Five

MAD ELEPHANT

After a failed attempt to assassinate the Buddha with the help of Ajatasattu, Devadatta decided he would have to kill the Buddha himself. When the Blessed One was at Rajagraha, he usually stayed at the Gijjakuta, a small rocky hill. Devadatta climbed the Gijjakuta, and when he saw the Buddha walking up and down at the foot of the hill, he sent a large rock tumbling down. Just before the rock reached the Buddha, it hit another rock that diverted it, although a splinter hit the Buddha injuring his foot.

The Buddha looked up and, seeing Devadatta, remarked with pity, "Foolish man, you have done many unwholesome deeds for harming the Buddha."

Sometime later, Devadatta went into the royal stables, where a huge and fierce elephant named Nalagiri was kept. He approached the mahouts and, flaunting his royal patronage, managed to convince them to release the elephant in the Buddha's path.

The next day, the Blessed One with his group of monks walked through the streets of Rajagraha to collect alms. As they turned through a corner into a narrow street, Nalagiri the elephant was set loose. The mad elephant charged down the street straight towards the Buddha and his group. People ran to get out of the way and climbed onto the roofs of the houses to see what would happen. The monks called the Buddha to turn back, but he continued to walk on calmly.

As the tusker approached the Blessed One, people were filled with fear awaiting something terrible to happen. To their surprise, the Buddha was able to suffuse the giant with his thoughts of loving-kindness so much that Nalagiri quietened down, allowing the Blessed One to approach him and gently stroke his forehead.

This confrontation caused a sensation in Rajagraha, and for weeks people went around the city singing this praise:
Some are tamed by goad and whips,
But the elephant by the great sage was tamed
By loving kindness, without sword or stick.

And so Devadatta did not succeed in his plans. Still possessed by hatred and abandoned by many of his disciples, he fell fatally ill and repented. Devadatta entreated those who had remained with him to take him to the Buddha, saying, "Take me, children, take me to him; though I have done evil to him, I am his relative. For the sake of our relationship the Buddha will save me." And they obeyed, although reluctantly.

Twenty-Six

ONE REASON

At the same time, King Ajatasattu suffering greatly from the pangs of his conscience went to the Blessed One and sought guidance and peace in his distress. The Buddha received Ajatasattu kindly and taught him the way of liberation.

The king asked, "O Blessed One, can you show me any benefits of the monk's life that can be seen here and now?"

The Buddha replied by asking him, "If you had a slave who ran away and became a monk and later, on finding out where he was, would you have him arrested and brought back?"

"Certainly not!" replied the king, "On the contrary, I would stand up for him, respect him and offer to provide him with his needs."

"Well, that is one of the benefits of being a monk that can be seen here and now."

Twenty-Seven

ANGULIMALA

The King of Kosala had an adviser called Bhaggawa whose job was to read the stars, advise about the best time to embark on various projects and ward off evil influences with spells and mantras. Bhaggawa was filled with joy when his wife gave birth to a boy, but when the baby's horoscope was drawn up, his joy turned to dread. The horoscope indicated that the boy would grow up with criminal tendencies. Filled with superstitious fear, the parents decided to name the boy Ahimsaka meaning 'harmless' and hoped that this would counter the influence of the stars. The boy grew up good at his studies and obedient to his parents. Still, to ensure that the boy would never turn bad, Bhaggawa constantly stressed to Ahimsaka the importance of obedience and doing what he was told.

When Ahimsaka was old enough, his father sent him to a school in Takka Sila. In those days, young brahmins would go to Takka Sila and live in a teacher's house to learn traditional lore. Ahimsaka was the strongest, brightest and the most obedient child of all the children in the whole school. This earned him special attention from his teacher, but it also created jealousy in the other students. They decided to try to turn the teacher against Ahimsaka. According to their plan, they went one by one to the teacher and whispered

64

that his favourite student was trying to usurp his position.

At first the teacher dismissed this as nonsense, but gradually the seeds of doubt were sown. These seeds eventually sprouted into suspicion and the teacher became convinced of Ahimsaka's hostility toward him. 'This young man is strong in body and quite capable of doing me harm. I must get rid of him and make sure he never comes back,' he thought.

One day, the teacher called Ahimsaka and said, "You have successfully finished your studies. Now you must pay my tuition fee."

"Certainly," said Ahimsaka. " What do you demand as your fee?"

"You must bring me a thousand first fingers from the human hand."

"Surely you don't require this of me?" responded horrified Ahimsaka.

"You have taken from me and in return you must now do my bidding. Go now and bring a thousand fingers. And remember not to bring two fingers from the same person."

The teacher's hope was, of course, that in the process of carrying out this task Ahimsaka would be killed and never seen again.

The unhappy student returned to Kosala and went to live in the Jalani forest. Reluctantly at first, but later without compunction, he began waylaying lone travellers, killing them, cutting off one of their fingers and living off the possessions he stole. Ahimsaka made a garland out of the finger bones and soon became known as Angulimala meaning 'necklace of fingers.' Eventually Angulimala accumulated 999 fingers.

His parents came to hear that the murderer whom everyone was talking about was their own son. Embarrassed and ashamed, the old Bhaggawa disowned his son. His mother could not bring herself to do so and she planned to go into the Jalani forest and try to speak to her son.

Just when it appeared that Angulimala, being very impatient to finally pay off his debt, might even kill his own mother, the Buddha looked around the world to see if anybody needed help. When he saw Angulimala and his mother, the Blessed One set out towards the forest.

As the Buddha walked along the road, groups of travellers passed him, and as they did, they warned him not to continue alone because of the danger. He simply smiled and continued on his way. When Angulimala saw the Buddha, he thought, 'This is wonderful. Here is an ascetic travelling alone. I will kill him.'

Seizing his sword and shield, Angulimala emerged from the jungle and began to chase after the Buddha, but although he ran as fast as he could, he could not catch up with the Buddha, who only walked. He put on a burst of speed but still could not get near the Buddha.

Utterly bewildered, he shouted out, "Stand still, ascetic!"

The Buddha turned around, looked at him and replied, "I am still. Why don't you be still also?"

Even more bewildered, Angulimala asked, "What do you mean, ascetic?"

"I am still in that I harm no living being. You kill, therefore, you are not still," replied the Buddha.

The terrible things he had done and the wretchedness of his life dawned on Angulimala and he broke down and sobbed. He threw down his weapons, bowed at the Buddha's feet and asked to become a monk. The Buddha ordained him and together they set out for Sravastti.

Angulimala led a life of simplicity and solitude and under the Buddha's guidance eventually attained enlightenment. But even then, many remembered his terrible past, and people shunned him. Often Angulimala would return from his alms round with no food, and sometimes people would throw stones at him.

The Buddha comforted him, saying, "You must endure this, Angulimala. You must silently endure this. This is a result of the deeds you have done previously."

One day, while wandering door-to-door for alms in Sravastti, Angulimala came across a young woman undergoing a difficult labor. He was deeply moved on seeing the woman's plight and hurried back to the Buddha and asked him what to do to ease the woman's pain.

And the Blessed One said, "In that case, Angulimala, go into Sravastti and say to the woman, 'Sister, since I was born, I do not recall that I have ever intentionally deprived a living being of life. By this truth, may you be well and may your infant be well!'

To this Angulimala replied, "Would not I be telling a deliberate lie, for I have intentionally deprived many living beings of life?"

"Then, Angulimala, go into Sravastti and say to that woman, 'Sister, since I was born with the noble birth, I do not recall that I have ever intentionally deprived a living being of life. By this truth, may you be well and may your infant be well!' "

With this Angulimala hurried back to Sravastti and told that woman, "Sister, since I was born with the noble birth, I do not recall that I have ever deprived a living being of life. By this truth, may you be well and may your infant be well!"

And only when he said this benediction, the woman safely gave birth without any severe pain. After this event, Angulimala was seen to bring safety to people, and the people also started to approach him and provide him with alms food. At last, his earlier name 'Ahimsaka' fully befitted him.

Twenty-Eight

SPIRITUAL POWERS

Once the Blessed One was dwelling at Veluvana, the bamboo grove near Rajagraha.

At that time, Sariputta and Moggallana were living at the Kapotakandara monastery. And one moonlit night, while sitting with a lately shaven head in the open air, Sariputta fell into a mystical trance.

Now it so happened that two yakshas, local demons, were travelling from one region to the other. And when they saw Sariputta in a state of trance, sitting with a lately shaven head, the first yaksha said to the second yaksha, "It occurs to me, friend, to give this monk a blow on the head."

The second yaksha replied, "Enough, friend, do not strike the monk. He is very powerful and mighty in spiritual strength."

In all, three times did the first yaksha told of his resolve to strike Sariputta, and each time his friend warned him not to do so. Ultimately, the first yaksha, not heeding his friend's warning, delivered a blow on the head of Sariputta; such a blow that could have fallen an elephant.

But Sariputta remained unmoved, drowned in his mystical trance.

As soon as the wicked yaksha had struck Sariputta, he himself was reduced to ashes. Witnessing this, the second yaksha fled in fear.

Now, Moggallana was able to see all of this with this spiritual eye. And he went to the place where Sariputta was and said, "I trust, brother, that you are at ease, that you are doing well, that there is no pain."

By this time Sariputta had come out of his trance and was able to respond, saying, "I am at ease, brother Moggallana, and I am doing well, but I feel a slight pain in my head."

"How strange and marvellous is it, brother Sariputta! How great is your spiritual power and might, brother Sariputta! Just now, a certain yaksha delivered a blow on your head, a blow which could have fallen an elephant," said Moggallana in excitement.

Replied Sariputta, "It is wonderful, brother Moggallana! How great is your spiritual power and mind, brother Moggallana, that you saw a yaksha at all. I did not see even a mud-sprite."

The Buddha, hearing this far-off conversation with his spiritual ear, uttered this verse:
He whose heart, like a rock unshaken stands,
Who is passion free, not angry with the angry.
He whose heart is thus trained,
How shall pain come to such a one?

Twenty-Nine

MIRACLES FORBIDDEN

Once a householder in Rajagraha erected a long pole in front of his house and placed a precious sandalwood bowl decorated with jewels. Then he made a proclamation that if a monk of any sect was able to bring the bowl down without using a ladder, stick or a hook or without climbing the pole, that monk could take the precious bowl as a reward for his feat.

At that time, Moggallana along with some fellow monks happened to pass by the pole. They noticed the bowl hung over it and learned about the householder's proclamation.

As Moggallana was well-known for his supernormal powers, his fellow monk Kassapa urged him to prove the superiority of the Buddha's Sangha by bringing down the bowl. Moggallana refused, saying that Kassapa himself possessed sufficient powers to do it.

So Kassapa simply stretched out his hands, and the bowl miraculously landed on his palms. Witnessing this supernormal feat, the people erupted in joy, and they went to the Buddha praising his monks and telling him everything about Kassapa's feat.

The Blessed One was not at all amused to hear what had happened. He went to Kassapa and, breaking the bowl to pieces, forbade his disciples to perform miracles of any kind.

Soon many monks were staying in the Vajji territory during a famine. And one of the monks proposed that they should praise one another to the householders of the village, saying, "This monk is a saint; he has seen celestial visions; that monk possesses supernatural gifts; he can work miracles." On hearing this, the villagers said, "It is fortunate for us that such saints are spending the rainy season here." And they gave food abundantly to the monks who avoided suffering from the famine.

When the Blessed One heard it, he called the monks together and asked them, "Tell me, when does a monk cease to be a monk?"

And Sariputta replied, "An ordained monk must not commit any dishonourable act. The monk who commits a dishonourable act is no longer a disciple of the Buddha. An ordained disciple must not take except what has been given him. And lastly, an ordained disciple must not knowingly and malignantly deprive any harmless creature of life, not even an earthworm or an ant. The disciple who knowingly and malignantly deprives any harmless creature of its life is no longer a disciple of the Buddha. These are the three great prohibitions."

Then the Blessed One said, "There is another great prohibition which I declare to you. An ordained disciple must not boast of any superhuman perfection. The disciple, who boasts of superhuman perfection with evil intent and covetousness, be it celestial visions or miracles, is no longer a disciple of the Buddha. He who attempts to perform miracles has not understood the doctrine of Dharma."

The Buddha knew that the display of psychic powers could have quite an effect upon people and not always a positive one. Those who displayed such powers could easily be spoiled by the adulation they received, while those who saw such powers displayed often gave unthinking devotion to those who had them. Still, he also realized that psychic powers could sometimes be put to good use. On one occasion, some thieves attacked a house and kidnapped two children. When the monk Pilindavaccha heard of this, he used his psychic powers to bring the children back. When other monks accused him of breaking the rule, the Buddha declared Pilindavaccha innocent of any offence because he had used his powers out of compassion.

Thirty

NUN KHEMA

One of the Buddha's greatest disciples was a nun named Khema. She was a chief of nuns and well-respected for her penetrative insight and wisdom. The sutras describe that she was on the path of attaining knowledge through many reincarnations. One of such stories recounts that in one of the former lives, Khema was born in the city Hamsavati ruled by Padumuttara. One day, she had her hair cut off and bartered it for gifts, which she gave to the monks, uttering the prayer, "Hereafter, at some time when a Buddha appears in the world, may I become full of wisdom like you."

Only because Khema had already purified her heart and perfected it in these virtues in many past lives, she had such pure and tranquil emotions that she could accept the ultimate teaching in the twinkling of an eye and was reborn in the time of the Buddha in the royal family in the city of Sagala. When she came of age, she entered the household of King Bimbisara.

King Bimbisara asked Khema to go to the monastery at Jetavana to pay homage to the Buddha, but she had heard that the Buddha always spoke disparagingly about beauty and therefore avoided him. Knowing this, the king asked his musicians to sing praises of the monastery. These songs roused Khema's curiosity, and she went to the monastery.

Aware of her thoughts when she arrived, the Buddha created a celestial nymph who fanned him while he was teaching the Dharma. Only Khema perceived the heavenly maiden and saw her fade and wither away; in the end only a corpse was left to be seen. Khema instantly realized the truth of impermanence. The Blessed One then told her, "O Khema, look carefully at this decayed body which is now only a skeleton of bones and had always been subject to disease and decay. Look carefully at the body which the foolish cherish so much. Look at the worthlessness of this young woman's beauty."

Then the Buddha uttered this verse:
  Beings who are infatuated with lust
  Fall back into the stream of the craving they create,
  And they resemble a spider trapped in the web it has spun.
  The wise, having vanquished craving,
  Do the way with determination and leave all ill behind.

Having listened attentively, Khema understood the doctrine of Dharma and thought to herself, 'I will ask permission to forsake the world myself.' Making obeisance to the Master, she returned to the palace and asked the king for permission to forsake the world. King Bimbisara granted her request and sent her in a golden palanquin to the nunnery, where she should dwell.

Soon Khema became known for her great wisdom, and the Blessed One assigned her the chief place among those who are full of knowledge, saying, "Khema is matchless amongst the nuns in wisdom, and she knows how to differentiate the right way from the wrong way." Then the Buddha spoke this verse:
  The one I call a Brahmana,
  who is wise and profound in his knowledge,
  who knows the right way from the wrong way,

and who has attained the highest goal of an Arhat.

Thirty-One

CINCA'S DECEIT

Once when the Blessed One dwelt at Sravastti, several brahmans conspired to falsely accuse the Buddha of sleeping with a woman and making her pregnant. They found an attractive, young brahmana woman named Cinca and told her that the Buddha had caused a rapid decline in the faith of their ancestors by luring many young men to become his disciples. Anxious to protect her faith, Cinca agreed to the plan.

Every day she went to Jetavana dressed in a beautiful sari and carrying a fresh bouquet of flowers. She did not arrive in time for the Dharma talks but waited outside the Dharma hall as people left to return home. At first whenever anyone asked her where she was going or what she was doing, she only smiled. After several days, she answered coyly, "I am going where I am going." After several weeks of such vague comments, she began to answer, "I am going to visit Teacher Gautama." And finally, she was heard to exclaim, "Sleeping at Jetavana is delightful!"

Such words burned the ears of many people. Some laypeople began to feel doubts and suspicions, but no one said anything. One day, Cinca came to one of the Buddha's Dharma talks. Her belly was noticeably round. In the middle of the Buddha's discourse, she stood up and loudly said, "Teacher Gautama! You speak eloquently about the Dharma. You are held in high esteem. But you care nothing for this poor woman made pregnant by you. The child I carry is your own. Are you going to take responsibility for your own child?"

A wave of shock passed through the community. Everyone looked up at the Buddha. The Buddha only smiled calmly and replied, "Only you and I can know whether or not your claims are true."

The Buddha's calm smile made Cinca feel uneasy, but she retorted, "That's right, only you and I know whether my claims are true."

The community could no longer suppress their astonishment. Several people stood up in anger. Cinca suddenly felt afraid the people would beat her. She looked for a way to escape, but in her panic, she ran into a post and stumbled. As she strained to stand back up, a large round block of wood fell from where it was tied onto her abdomen and landed on her foot. Her stomach was now perfectly flat.

A sigh of relief rose from the crowd. Several people began laughing, and others derided Cinca. Nun Khema stood up and gently assisted Cinca out of the hall. When the two women were gone, the Buddha resumed his Dharma talk as if nothing had happened.

The Buddha spoke, "O Monks, the Way of Enlightenment can tear down the walls of ignorance, just as light can disperse the shadows. The Four Noble Truths, Impermanence, Non-self, the Seven Factors of Awakening, the Three Gates, and the Noble Eightfold Path have all been proclaimed to the world like a lion's roar, dispelling countless false doctrines and narrow views. The lion is the king of the beasts. When he leaves his den, he stretches and gazes out over all the directions. Before seeking his prey, he lets forth a mighty roar that causes the other creatures to tremble and flee. Birds fly high; crocodiles dive beneath the water, and foxes slip into their holes. Even village elephants, decked in fancy belts and ornaments and shaded by golden parasols, run away at the sound of that roar.

"O Monks, the proclamation of the Way of Enlightenment is like that lion's roar! False doctrines fear and tremble. When it is proclaimed, all those who have long sought false security in ignorance and forgetfulness must awaken, celestial beings as well as human beings. When a person sees the dazzling truth, he exclaims, 'We embraced dangerous views for so long, taking the impermanent to be permanent, and believing in the existence of a separate self. We took suffering to be pleasure and looked at the temporary as if it were eternal. We mistook the false for the true. Now the time has come to tear down all the walls of forgetfulness and false views.'

"The Way of Enlightenment allows humanity to remove the thick veil of false views. When an enlightened person appears, the Way echoes like the majestic sound of the rising tide. When the tide rises, all false views are swept away. People are easily caught by four traps. The first is attachment to sensual desires. The second is attachment to narrow views. The third is doubt and suspicion. The fourth is a false view of self. The Way of Enlightenment helps people overcome the four great traps."

The next day in the main hall, Ananda repeated the Buddha's Dharma talk. He named it Sutra of the Lion's Roar.

Thirty-Two

CRISIS IN KOSAMBI

Kosambi was a large city situated on the banks of the Yamuna River. Because it was at a junction of several routes, it had become a centre for trade and commerce. One of the city's most wealthy merchant, Ghosita, and his close friends had heard about the Buddha. One day while in Sravastti on business, they went to meet the Buddha and invited him to come to Kosambi. Each friend offered the Buddha a pleasure park which gradually grew into monasteries. Ghosita's park, which was just inside the east gate of Kosambi, came to be known as Ghositarama and grew into a great centre for the study of Dharma.

The Buddha stayed in Kosambi on several occasions and delivered many discourses there. His most famous disciple there was the woman Khujjuttara. She was a slave working in King Udena's harem, and as Queen Samavati and the other women were not allowed to leave the harem, one of her jobs was to run errands for the queen and the other women in the harem. One day, Khujjuttara went to the garden to buy flowers for the queen, and while there, she heard the Buddha teaching the Dharma and understood it. On returning to the harem, she told the queen about the Dharma. Delighted by what she heard, the queen thereafter sent her regularly to listen to the

Buddha so she could repeat what she heard. In this manner, Khujjuttara
became an expert in Dharma. In fact, the Buddha called her the most deeply
learned of all his female lay disciples. All the discourses in the Itivuttaka, one
of the most important books in the Tipitaka, were preserved by Khujjuttara
and taught by her to the monks.

It was at Kosambi that the first serious crisis occurred in the Sangha. Two
monks were living together in the same hut. The first of these monks was
an expert in monastic discipline and was also conscientious and sincere.
One day, this monk went to the toilet and, when finished, failed to refill
the water pot. His companion scolded him and a bitter argument gradually
developed. The second monk insisted that the first had broken a rule, and
the first insisted that he had not. Eventually all the monks in Kosambi got
involved, taking either one side or the other, and the whole community
became quarrelsome and contentious. The Buddha tried, again and again,
to bring about a reconciliation but to no avail. So he decided to show his
disapproval of their unruly behaviour by walking out on them. He took his
robe and bowl and left for more congenial surroundings, saying this stanza:

"He abused me, he hit me,
He oppressed me, he robbed me."
Those who continue to hold such thoughts
Never still their hatred.
Those who do not hold such thoughts
Soon still their hatred.
For in this world
Hatred is never appeased by more hatred.
It is love that conquers hatred.
This is an eternal law.

Not far from Kosambi there was a park called the Eastern Bamboo Grove,
and the Buddha decided to go there. After staying at the park for a while, the
Buddha left and went to Sravastti. Meanwhile, back in Kosambi, the people
decided to withdraw their support from the monks. Gradually, the monks

found less reason to carry on their dispute. As their tempers cooled down, they began to feel ashamed of themselves. So a delegation of monks went to Sravastti to see the Buddha and ask for his forgiveness, which he gave, thus bringing the Kosambi dispute to an end.

Thirty-Three

VISAKHA

Visakha, a wealthy woman in the city of Sravastti with many children and grandchildren, had given generously to the Sangha and was the first in Northern Kosala to become a matron of the lay sisters.

When the Blessed One stayed at Sravastti, Visakha went up to where the Blessed One was and tendered him an invitation to take his meal at her house, which the Blessed One accepted. As heavy rain fell during the night and the next morning, the monks doffed their robes to keep them dry and let the rain fall upon their bodies.

The next day, when the Blessed One had finished his meal, Visakha took her seat at his side and said, "O Blessed One, please grant me eight boons."

Said the Blessed One, "What are the boons you are requesting, Visakha?"

Visakha replied, "Master, I desire through all my life long to bestow robes for the rainy season on the Sangha, and food for incoming monks, and food for outgoing monks, and food for the sick, and food for those who take care of the sick, and medicine for the sick and a constant supply of rice milk for the Sangha, and bathing robes for the nuns, the sisters."

Said the Buddha, "What circumstances made you, Visakha, ask these eight boons?"

Visakha replied, "I gave the command, Master, to my maidservant to go and announce to the brotherhood that the meal is ready. And the maid went, but when she came to the vihara, she observed that the monks had doffed their robes while it was raining. Then she thought that these were not monks but naked ascetics letting the rain fall on them. So she returned to me and reported accordingly. Because of this circumstance I desire to provide the Sangha with special garments for use in the rainy season.

"As to my second wish, Master, an incoming monk, not being able to take the direct roads and not knowing the place where food can be procured, comes on his way tired out by seeking for alms. Because of this circumstance I desire to provide the Sangha with food for incoming monks. Thirdly, an outgoing monk, while seeking about for alms, may be left behind or may arrive too late at the place where he desires to go and will set out on the road in weariness. Fourthly, if a sick monk does not obtain suitable food, his sickness may increase, and he may die. Fifthly, a monk who is taking care of the sick will lose his opportunity of going out to seek food for himself. Sixthly, if a sick monk does not obtain suitable medicines, his sickness may increase, and he may die. Seventhly, I have heard that the Blessed One has praised rice-milk, because it gives readiness of mind and dispels hunger and thirst; it is wholesome for the healthy as nourishment and for the sick as a medicine. Therefore I desire to provide the Sangha with a constant supply of rice-milk.

"Finally, the nuns are in the habit of bathing in the river Achiravati with the courtesans, at the same landing-place, and naked. And the courtesans ridicule the nuns, saying, 'What is the good of you maintaining chastity when you are young? When you are old, maintain chastity then; this way you will obtain both worldly pleasure and religious consolation.' These are the circumstances, O Blessed One."

The Buddha said, "It is well, Visakha. You have done well in asking these eight boons with such advantages. Charity bestowed upon those who are worthy of it is like good seeds sown on a good soil that yields an abundance of fruits. But alms given to those who are yet under the oppressive yoke of the passions are like seeds deposited in a bad soil. The passions of the receiver of the alms choke, as it were, the growth of merits."

And the Blessed One thanked Visakha by uttering this verse:

O noble woman of an upright life,
Disciple of the Blessed One, you give
Generously in purity of heart.
You spread joy, assuage pain,
And verily your gift will be a blessing
As well to many others as to you.

Thirty-Four

ANNOUNCEMENT

When the Blessed One went to Beluva, a place near Vesali, to spend the rainy season there, a dire sickness and sharp pains fell upon him. As the Buddha bore his ailments mindfully without complaint, Mara, the Evil One, came and said the same words as he did when the Blessed One was resting under the Bodhi tree, "Be greeted, the Enlightened One. You have attained the highest bliss. Now it is time for you to enter into the final stage of liberation."

When Mara thus had spoken, the Blessed One said, "Rejoice, O Evil One! The final extinction of the Buddha shall take place soon."

When Ananda heard about this, he addressed the Blessed One, "Vouchsafe, Master, to remain with us for the good and the happiness of the great multitudes, out of pity for the world, for the good and the gain of mankind!"

Said the Blessed One, "Enough now, Ananda, do not beseech the Buddha!"

When the second time Ananda besought the Blessed One in the same words, he received from the Blessed One the same reply. And again, when the third time, Ananda besought the Blessed One to live longer, the Blessed One said,

"Do you have faith, Ananda?"

Replied Ananda, "I have, Master!"

Then the Blessed One continued, "If you have faith in the wisdom of the Buddha, why then, Ananda, do you keep beseeching the Buddha? Have I not previously declared to you that it is in the very nature of all compound things that they must be dissolved again? We must separate ourselves from all things near and dear to us and must leave them. How then, Ananda, can it be possible for me to remain since everything that is born, or brought into being, and organized, contains within itself the inherent necessity of dissolution? How, then, can it be possible that this body of mine should not be dissolved? No such condition can exist! And this mortal existence, Ananda, has been relinquished, cast away, renounced, rejected, and abandoned by the Buddha."

The Blessed One continued, "Go now, Ananda, and assemble the monks."

Then the Buddha proceeded to the assembly, sat down on the mat spread out for him and addressed the monks, saying, "O Monks, you to whom the truth has been made known, having thoroughly made yourselves masters of it, practice it, meditate upon it, and spread it, so that pure knowledge may last long and be perpetuated, so that it may continue for the good and happiness of the great multitudes, out of pity for the world, and to the good and gain of all living beings!

"He who lets his heart go loose without restraint shall not attain the final liberation. Therefore, must we hold the heart in check, retire from worldly excitements and seek the tranquility of mind. Eat your food to satisfy your hunger and drink to satisfy your thirst. Satisfy the necessities of life, like the butterfly that sips the flower without destroying its fragrance or its texture. Practice the earnest meditations I have taught you. Continue in the great struggle against sin. Be strong in moral powers. Let the organs of your spiritual sense be quick. When the seven kinds of wisdom enlighten your mind, you will find the noble, eightfold path that leads to enlightenment. Behold, O Monks, the final extinction of the Buddha will take place soon. Seek what is permanent and work out your liberation with diligence."

Thirty-Five

THE BUDDHA'S FAREWELL

Not long after his final announcement, the Blessed One proceeded with a great company of the monks to the sala grove of the Mallas. Upon arrival, he asked Ananda to prepare a couch with its head to the north, between the twin sala trees. As the Blessed One laid himself down, the twin sala trees became full of bloom with flowers and heavenly songs came wafted from the skies.

When Ananda became filled with wonder that the Blessed One was thus honored, the Blessed One said, "Not by such events, Ananda, is the Buddha rightly honored, held sacred, or revered. But the devout man, who continually fulfills the greater and the lesser duties, walking according to the precepts, rightly honors, holds sacred and reveres the Buddha with the worthiest homage. Therefore, Ananda, fulfill the greater and the lesser duties with diligence and walk according to the precepts to honor the Master."

Then Ananda went into the monastery, stood leaning against the doorpost in grieve, and thought, 'Alas! I remain still but a learner, one who has yet to work out his own perfection. And the Master is about to pass away from me!'

The Blessed One asked the monks to call Ananda and addressed him, "Enough, Ananda! Do not be troubled! Have I not already, on former occasions, told you that it is in the very nature of all things most near and dear to us that we must separate from them and leave them? My journey is drawing to its close. I have reached the sum of my days; I am turning eighty years of age. Just as a wornout cart can not be made to move along without much difficulty, so this body can only be kept going with much additional care."

Ananda suppressed his tears and said to the Blessed One, "Deep darkness reigned for want of wisdom; the world of sentient creatures was groping for want of light; then the Buddha lit up the lamp of wisdom, and now it will be extinguished again."

The Buddha responded, "O Ananda, be a lamp unto yourself, be a refuge to yourself. Take yourself to no external refuge. Hold fast to the truth as a lamp; hold fast to the truth as a refuge. Those who shall be lamps unto themselves, relying upon themselves only and not relying upon any external help, but holding fast to the truth as their lamp, and seeking their salvation in the truth alone, it is they, Ananda, who shall reach the very topmost height!"

II

TEACHINGS

"A teaching I here give unto you, so that you may understand the meaning of the matter." - Gautama Buddha

Thirty-Six

THE MUSTARD SEED

Kisa Gotami was the wife of a wealthy man living in the city of Sravastti. She had an only son, and when he died, Kisa became desperate to revive him. In her grief she carried the dead child to all her neighbors, asking them for medicine to cure the child.

And the people said, "She has lost her senses. The boy is dead."

At last, Kisa Gotami met an old man who said, "I cannot give you medicine for your child, but I know a physician who can."

With a glimpse of hope, the distraught mother asked, "Please tell me, who is it?"

The kind-hearted man replied, "Go to the Buddha who dwells at Jetavana."

Kisa Gotami hurried to the Jeta's Grove Monastery, and on arriving there she found the Buddha in the middle of a discourse.

And she cried out, "O Blessed One, give me the medicine that will cure my boy."

The Buddha stopped his discourse and noticed that the boy was dead. Seeing the distraught condition of the mother, he said, "This can be done, but I need a handful of mustard seed."

When Kisa Gotami in her joy promised to procure it, the Buddha added, "The mustard seed must be taken from a house where no one has lost a child, husband, parent, or any relative."

Thus Kisa Gotami went from house to house, and the people pitied her, saying, "Here is the mustard seed; take it!" But when she asked, "Did a son or daughter, a father or mother, die in your family?" The householders answered, "Alas, the living are few, but the dead are many. Do not remind us of our deepest grief."

And there was no house where a beloved one had not died.

Kisa Gotami became weary and hopeless. Overcome with emotion, she sat down at the wayside and considered the fate of humans. Then she went outside of the city, carried her son to the burning-ground, and said, "Dear little son, I thought that you alone had been overtaken by this thing which men call death. But you are not the only one death has overtaken. This is a law common to all mankind." She uttered the following stanza:

No village law, no law of market-town,
No law of a single house is this,
Of all the world and all the Worlds of Gods,
This only is the law - all things are impermanent.

Then she returned to the Buddha, took the threefold refuge and found comfort in the Dharma. The Buddha said, "The life of mortals in this world is troubled, brief and combined with pain. Those that have been born can not avoid dying. After reaching old age, there is death. This is the nature of all living beings. As ripe fruits are in danger of falling, so mortals when born are always in danger of death. Both young and adult fall into the power of death; all are subject to death."

Thirty-Seven

EVERY STEP

Once a young man came to the Buddha and asked, "O Master, I have this doubt in my mind. Many people come to listen to you. Many of them are asking you how to find the right path. Do all these people reach enlightenment? If you are so powerful, so enlightened and compassionate, why don't you just take us to the final goal?"

The Buddha asked the young man, "Where do you live?"

"In Sravastti," replied the young man, "but I was born and brought up in Rajagraha, the capital of Magadha. Every now and then I go there to see my relatives and friends."

"Then you know the way to Rajagraha well," said the Buddha.

"Certainly! I can go there even blindfolded."

"Do people, now and then, ask you the way to Rajagraha?"

"Yes, and I guide them clearly. I tell them exactly how to get there. First go towards the East, then take the way to Benares and from there go straight ahead till Gaya. From Gaya you can easily find the way to Rajagraha."

"But do all the people to whom you give those directions reach Rajagraha?"

"How is that possible, Master? Only those who follow the way to the end will reach the city."

"So it is with liberation; so it is with the doctrine. I explain the way to freedom as clearly as possible. But if they do not take the necessary steps, if they remain where they are, how can they reach the goal? Indeed, this is the path I took to reach enlightenment; however, one can not carry another to the final goal. Each must walk the path. Each step brings us closer to the path," said the Buddha.

Thirty-Eight

GUARD THE SIX QUARTERS

While the Blessed One was staying at the bamboo grove near Rajagraha, he once met on his way Sigala, a householder, who clasping his hands turned to the four quarters of the world, to the sky above, and to the earth below. The Blessed One, knowing that this was done according to the traditional religious superstition to avert evil, asked Sigala, "Why do you perform these strange ceremonies?"

And Sigala asked, "Do you think it is strange that I protect my home against the influences of demons? I know that you can tell me, Master, whom people call the Blessed Buddha, that incantations are of no avail and possess no saving power. But know that in performing this rite I honor and keep sacred my father's words."

Then the Buddha said, "Sigala, it is good to honor and keep sacred the words of your father; and it is your duty to protect your home, your wife, your children, and your children's children against the hurtful influences of evil spirits. I find no fault with the performance of your father's rite. But I find that you do not understand the ceremony. Let me, who now speaks to you as a spiritual father and loves you no less than your parents did, explain to you the meaning of the six directions.

"To guard your home by mysterious ceremonies is not sufficient; you must guard it by good deeds. Turn to your parents in the East, to your teachers in the South, to your wife and children in the West, to your friends in the North, and regulate the zenith of your religious relations above your, and the nadir of your servants below you. Such is the religion your father wants you to have, and the performance of the ceremony shall remind you of your duties."

On hearing this, Sigala looked up to the Blessed One with reverence for his father and said, "Truly, you are the Buddha, the Blessed One, the holy teacher. I never knew what I was doing, but now I know. You have revealed to me the truth that was hidden as one who brings a lamp into the darkness."

Thirty-Nine

THE POISONOUS SNAKE

Some thieves stole a large sum of money and came to a field to divide the stolen property among themselves. One packet of money, having been dropped from one of the thieves, was left behind unnoticed.

Early in the morning on that day, the Buddha was walking through the same field accompanied by Ananda. The farmer, who was plowing the field at the time, saw the Buddha and paid obeisance to him.

The Buddha then saw the packet of money and said to Ananda, "Ananda, look at that very poisonous snake," and Ananda replied, "Master, yes, it is, indeed, a very poisonous snake!"

Then, both the Buddha and Ananda continued their way.

The farmer, hearing them, went to find out if there really was a snake and found the packet of money. He took the packet and hid it. The property owners, coming after the thieves visited the field and tracing the farmer's footprints, found the packet of money.

They beat the farmer and took him to the king, who ordered his men to kill the farmer. On being taken to the cemetery, where he were to be killed, the farmer kept on repeating, "Ananda, look at that very poisonous snake. Master, yes, it is, indeed, a very poisonous snake!"

When the king's men heard this dialogue between the Buddha and Ananda being repeated all the way, they were puzzled and took him to the king. The king deduced that the farmer was calling upon the Buddha as a witness, and therefore, he was taken to the presence of the Buddha. After hearing from the Buddha everything that had happened in the morning, the king remarked, "If he had not been able to call upon the Buddha as a witness of his innocence, this man would have been killed."

Then the Buddha said, "A wise man should not do anything that he would repent after doing it." He then continued with this verse:

That deed is not well done,
If one regrets having done it,
And if, with a tearful face,
One has to weep as a result of that deed.

Forty

THE PEAKED ROOF

Once the Blessed One said to the merchant Anathapindika, "Householder, when the mind has failed, bodily, verbal, and mental actions fail. One whose bodily, verbal, and mental deeds fail will not have a good transition after the death. Suppose a house with a peaked roof is badly thatched; then the roof peak, the rafters, and the walls fail. So too, when the mind has failed, bodily, verbal, and mental actions fail. When the mind has not failed, bodily, verbal, and mental actions do not fail. One whose deeds of body, speech, and mind do not fail will have a good transition. Suppose a house with a peaked roof is well thatched; then the roof peak, the rafters, and the walls do not fail. So too, when the mind has not failed, bodily, verbal, and mental actions do not fail."

Forty-One

SEARCH

One time the Blessed One was heading to Uruvela. On the way he sat down in a grove to rest, and it happened that in that same grove was a party of thirty friends who were enjoying themselves, and while they were celebrating, some of their goods were stolen. Then the whole party searched for the thief, and, meeting the Blessed One sitting under a tree, they asked, "Monk, did you see the thief pass by with our goods?"

The Blessed One said, "Which is better for you, that you go in search for the thief or for yourselves?"

The young people exclaimed, "In search for ourselves!"

The Blessed One said, "Sit down and I will teach you."

And the whole party sat down, and they listened eagerly to the words of the Buddha.

Forty-Two

OLD AGE

Once a number of brahmins, old, burdened with years, coming to the last stage, approached the Blessed One and paid homage to him. When they had concluded their greetings and cordial talk, they sat down to one side and said to the Buddha, "We have heard, Master, that you do not pay homage to brahmins who are old, burdened with years, coming to the last stage; nor do you stand up for them or offer them a seat. This is not proper!"

The Buddha replied, "Age does not make one an elder. Even though someone is old— eighty, ninety, or a hundred years from birth— if he speaks at an improper time, speaks falsely, speaks what is unbeneficial, speaks words that are worthless, unreasonable and rambling, then he is reckoned as a foolish elder. But even though someone is young, with no gray hair, endowed with the blessing of youth, in the prime of life, speaks what is truthful, speaks what is beneficial, and if at a proper time he speaks words that are worth recording, reasonable, and succinct, then he is reckoned as a wise elder."

Forty-Three

THE WOMAN AT THE WELL

Ananda, having been sent by the Blessed One on a mission, passed by a well near a village. On seeing Pakati, a girl of the low caste, he asked her for water to drink. Pakati responded, "O Monk, I am too humble to give you water to drink. Do not ask any service of me or your holiness be contaminated, for I am of low caste."

And said Ananda, "I ask not for caste but for water."

The girl's heart leaped joyfully, and she gave Ananda water to drink.

Ananda thanked her and went away, but she followed him at a distance. Having heard that Ananda was a disciple of the Buddha, the girl hurried to the Blessed One and cried, "O Master, help me, let me live in the place where Ananda your disciple dwells, so that I may see him and minister to him, for I love Ananda."

The Blessed One understood the emotions of her heart and said, "Pakati, your heart is full of love, but you do not understand your own sentiments. It is not Ananda that you love, but his kindness. Accept, then, the kindness that you have seen him practice, and in the humility practice it unto others. There is great merit in the generosity of a king when he is kind to a slave, but there is greater merit in a slave when he ignores the wrongs which he suffers and cherishes kindness and goodwill to all mankind. If he ceases to hate his oppressors, then even when completely powerless to resist their usurpation, he will pity their arrogance with compassion.

"Blessed you are, Pakati, for you will be a model for noblemen and noblewomen. You are of low caste, but brahmins may learn a lesson from you. Serve from the path of justice and righteousness and you will outshine the royal glory of queens on the throne."

Forty-Four

ABUSIVE CROWD

At the time brahmins were often enraged that the Buddha was teaching the new ways and criticizing the traditional religion.

Once the Blessed One was passing through a brahmin village when the brahmins surrounded him screaming all sorts of threats and abuses.

The Buddha listened silently.

After they finished shouting, the Blessed One said to them, "If this is all you wanted to say to me, I would like to reach the place where people are waiting for me. But if this is not all you wanted to say to me, I will be returning here after a few days and I will have enough time to listen to all you want to say."

One man said, "Do you think we are saying something? We are condemning you. Don't you understand? Anybody else would become angry, and you are standing silently!"

Replied the Buddha to the angry crowd, "You have come a little too late. Ten years ago, I was a prince, a warrior, just as insane as you are. If you had come ten years ago, not a single person would have gone alive. But now I am no longer insane. I cannot react and I would like to ask you one question. In the last village people came with sweets and fruits to welcome my group of monks. As we take food only once a day, and we had already taken the food that day, we could not accept the sweets and fruits. Now I want to ask you - what must they have done with the sweets and fruits that they had brought as presents to us?"

One man answered, "They must have distributed the sweets in the village."

Then Buddha said, "So what will you do? I do not accept what you have brought the same way I did not accept those sweets and fruits. What are you going to do with all this dirt that you have come with? You will have to take it back to your homes and give it to your wives, to your children, to your neighbors."

Forty-Five

PURITY OF WATER

Once the Blessed One in the company of his monks was traversing the Malla country and came to Thuna, another brahmin village. The brahmin householders of Thuna, having heard that the Buddha was traversing the country in the company of his monks, filled up the well to the brim with grass and straw, so that these shaven monks, as they called them, should not obtain water to drink.

And the Blessed One sat down at the foot of a tree and said to Ananda, "Come, Ananda, fetch me some water from that well."

When these words had been spoken, Ananda said to the Blessed One, "That well, O Master, has been filled up to the brim with grass and straw by brahmin householders of Thuna, so that we may not obtain water to drink."

A second time the Blessed One said to Ananda, "Come, Ananda, fetch me some water." And Ananda yet again gave the same reply. But when a third time the Buddha said thus, Ananda agreed, and taking a bowl he went to the well.

When Ananda arrived at the well, he found that all the grass and straw had been removed and that it was full to the brim with clear, pure, translucent water. Then this thought occurred to Ananda, 'How astonishing, how marvellous is the mighty power and great strength of the Blessed One, that on my arrival all the grass and straw were removed and the well was full to the brim with clear, pure, translucent water.' And taking some water in the bowl, he brought it to the Blessed One.

On that occasion, the Buddha uttered this verse:

When there is water everywhere,
What need of a well?
When desire has been uprooted.
In search of what should a man wander?

Forty-Six

THE GIFT

When the Buddha observed the ways of society, he noticed that much misery came from malignity and foolish offences. So, one day, he addressed a gathering of people and said, "If a man foolishly does me wrong, I will return to him the protection of my ungrudging love; the more evil comes from him, the more good shall go from me; the fragrance of goodness always comes to me, and the harmful air of evil goes to him."

A foolish man, learning that the Buddha observed the principle of the great love which commends the return of good for evil, came and abused him. All this time the Buddha remained silent, pitying the man's folly.

When the man finished his abuse, the Buddha asked him, "Tell me, if a man declined to accept a present made to him, whom would it belong?"

"In that case, the present would belong to the man who offered it."

And the Blessed One said, "So you have railed at me, but I decline to accept your abuse and request you to keep it to yourself. Would it not be a source of misery to you? As the echo belongs to the sound and the shadow to the substance, so misery will overtake the evil-doer without fail."

The abuser made no reply, and the Buddha continued, "A wicked man who reproaches a virtuous one is like one who looks up and spits at heaven; the spittle soils not the heaven, but comes back and defiles the spitter. The slanderer is like one who flings dust at another when the wind is contrary; the dust returns to the one who threw it. The virtuous man can not be hurt, and the misery that the others would inflict comes back on themselves."

On hearing these words, the abuser went away ashamed. Later he returned and took the threefold refuge.

Forty-Seven

IS THERE GOD

One day, in the early morning mist, the Buddha was sitting in a garden quietly with his disciples. A man arrived and silently stood in the shadows. That man was a great devotee of Lord Rama. He had built many temples across the country and had devoted many years to the service of Lord Rama. He would always chant Rama's name and contemplate Rama's greatness. The man was old and close to his last years. But even after many years of dedicated spiritual effort he did not become enlightened.

He wanted to know for certain whether there was a god or not. When he heard about the Buddha, he came to get his doubt cleared. When he felt nobody would notice him talking to the Blessed One, he asked, "O Buddha, please tell me the truth! Is there a god?"

The Buddha from his intuition knew that man was a great devotee of Lord Rama, so he looked at that man with all seriousness and said, "No. There is no god".

The Buddha's disciples gathered in that garden were very relieved and joyous to finally know the truth that there was no god. They all started muttering between them, sharing what the Buddha had just told. Whenever a disciple had asked that question before, the Blessed One would become silent. So previously they were in great confusion.

Shortly after, another man came to the garden to ask the Blessed One a question. He was a materialist and had been an atheist all his life. Moreover, he had convinced thousands of people that there was no god and even used to go to the priests and scholars and defeat them in religious arguments.

He too was getting old and a slight suspicion arose in him. Finally, he decided to find out the truth and asked the Buddha, "People say you are enlightened. Please tell me the truth! Is there a God?"

Knowing that this man was an atheist, the Buddha said with a firm voice, "Yes, there is a God."

On hearing these words, the Buddha's disciples once again were back to confusion.

The Blessed One had told each of them what they had to hear for them to get stronger on their spiritual quest.

Forty-Eight

ON REACTION

Once the Buddha was sitting under a tree talking to his disciples when one man came and spit on his face. The Blessed One wiped it off and asked that man, "What do you want to say next?"

The man became a little puzzled because he did not expect to hear back such a question. In the past, when he insulted people, they always became angry. But the Buddha was not angry.

The Buddha's disciples became angry, and Ananda said, "This is too much, and we cannot tolerate it. He has to be punished for it. Otherwise, everybody will start behaving this way."

The Buddha said to his disciples, "He has not offended me, but you are offending me. He is new, a stranger. He must have heard from people something about me: that this man is an atheist, a dangerous man who is throwing people off their track, a revolutionary, a corrupter. And he may have formed some idea, a notion of me. He has not spit on me; he has spit on his notion. He has spit on his own idea, his own mind. I am not part of it, and I can see that this poor man must have something else to say. Spitting

115

is a way of saying something, and that is why I am asking him. I am more offended by you because you know me, and you have lived for years with me, and still you react."

The man became even more puzzled. Confused, he returned home, but he could not sleep the whole night. Again and again, he was haunted by the experience. He could not explain to himself what had happened. The Buddha's behavior shattered his whole mind, his whole pattern, and his whole past.

The next morning he was back there. He threw himself at the Buddha's feet. The Blessed One asked him again, "What is next? This, too, is a way of saying something. When you come and touch my feet, you are saying something that cannot be said ordinarily."

The man looked at the Buddha and said, "Forgive me for what I did yesterday."

The Blessed One said, "Forgive? But I am not the same man to whom you did it. Ganges goes on flowing; it is never the same Ganges again. Every man is a river. The man you spit upon is no longer here. I look just like him, but I am not the same. The river has flowed so much. So I cannot forgive you because I have no grudge against you. And you are new also. I can see you are not the same man who came yesterday. That man was angry and spit, whereas you are bowing at my feet. How can you be the same man? Those two people, the man who spit and the man on whom he spits, both are no more."

Forty-Nine

THREE TYPES OF LISTENERS

One brahmin traveled from afar to meet the Buddha. When he met the Blessed One, he asked a question to which the Buddha responded that he would not be able to answer it at that moment.

"O Master, what is the reason for such a response?" asked brahmin and, wondering if the Buddha was busy, added, "Should I come back later?"

The Buddha replied, "I have enough time, but you will not be able to perceive the answer at this moment."

"There are three types of listeners," the Buddha continued, "The first listener's mind is like a pot with a big hole in it, wandering so much that all the knowledge leaks out immediately. The second listener's mind is like a pot turned upside down. No knowledge can enter that pot. In the third case, the listener's mind is full with other things; it can contain aggression, jealousy, and destruction of all kinds. One has mixed feelings about what is being said and cannot really understand it. The pot is not turned upside-down, and it doesn't have a hole in the bottom, but it has not been cleaned properly. You are the third type, so it is difficult for me to tell you anything at the moment.

You need to clean your mind first."

Fifty

BUTTER AND STONES

In those days, the brahmin priests used to charge money for a ritual prayer that promised to release a dead person's soul from hell and send it to heaven. At one point in the prayer, they struck an urn full of stones with a ritual hammer. According to their teaching, if the urn broke and the stones were released, it was a sign that the soul was also released.

Once a young man, distraught over his father's death, went to the Buddha, believing that the Buddha's teaching was a new form of religion, and asked him for a ritual which would release his father's soul. The Blessed One told him to obtain two ritual urns from the priests and fill one with butter and the other with stones. Believing he was about to get a more powerful ritual, the young man happily did so.

When the young man returned, the Buddha told him to place the urns carefully in the river so that the rim of the urn was just below the surface. Then he instructed him to recite the priests' usual prayer and strike both urns under the water with the hammer, then come back and describe what happened. And the young man performed the ritual as it was told to him.

On his return, the Buddha asked him to describe what he saw. The young man replied, "I saw nothing unusual. When I smashed the urns, the stones sank to the bottom of the river, and the butter was washed away on the river's surface."

The Buddha said, "Now please ask your priests to pray that the butter should sink, and the stones should float to the surface!"

Shocked by the obvious ridiculousness of the Buddha's request, the young man said, "No matter how much the priests pray, the stones will never float! The butter will not sink!"

The Buddha replied with a smile, "Exactly so. It is the same with your father. Whatever good wholesome actions he has done during his lifetime will make him rise towards heaven, and whatever bad unwholesome actions he has done will make him sink towards hell."

Fifty-One

THE BOAT

On one occasion, the Buddha was traveling with his disciples when they arrived at a river bed. They sat down patiently awaiting the boat to come so that they could go to the other side. As they were waiting, an old sage walked by them and walked over the water onto the other side.

The disciples were awe-struck, and when they were all in the boat, they started muttering among themselves. Finally, they asked the Buddha, "O Master, you are the Enlightened One! How is it that you did not walk on water?"

The Blessed One responded with a smile, "If I had walked across the water, what would you have done? I could have walked over the water, but how would that benefit you?"

Fifty-Two

THE LISTLESS FOOL

There was a rich and very old brahmin who, unmindful of the impermanence of earthly things and anticipating a long life, had built himself a large house. The Buddha wondered why a man so near his death had built a mansion with so many apartments. He sent Ananda to this wealthy brahmin to preach to him the four noble truths and the eightfold path of salvation. The brahmin showed Ananda his house and explained to him the purpose of its numerous chambers, but to the instruction of the Buddha's teachings he gave no heed.

Ananda said, "It is the habit of fools to say, 'I have children and wealth.' He who says so is not even master of himself; how can he claim possession of children, riches, and servants? Many are the anxieties of the worldly, but they know nothing of the changes of the future."

Soon after Ananda had left, the old man was stricken with apoplexy and fell dead. Then the Buddha said, "A fool, though he lives in the company of the wise, understands nothing, as a spoon tastes not the soup's flavor. He thinks of himself only and, unmindful of the advice of good counsellors, is unable to deliver himself."

Fifty-Three

ON ILLUMINATION

On one occasion, when the Buddha was residing in the country of Kausambi and preaching to the local people, he had met an educated brahmin.

This brahmin felt that he was unrivalled in the knowledge of scriptures. Being unable to find anyone equal to himself in an argument he was accustomed to carrying a lighted torch in his hand wherever he went.

Seeing this, the Buddha immediately called out to the brahmin, "Why are you carrying that torch?"

The brahmin replied, "The world is so dark that I carry this torch to light it up so far as I can. All men are so wrapped in ignorance, so I carry this torch to illumine them."

Then the Blessed One asked him again, "And are you so learned as to be acquainted with the four treatises called 'Vidyas' which occur amid the Sacred Books: the treatise on 'Literature'; the treatise on 'Heavenly Bodies and their Paths'; the treatise on 'Government'; and the treatise on 'Military Art'?"

The brahmin, being forced to confess he was unacquainted with these treatises, flung away his torch. Then the Buddha said, "If any man, whether he be learned or not, considers himself so great as to despise other men, he is like a blind man holding a candle—blind himself he illumines others."

Fifty-Four

VASAVADATTA, THE COURTESAN

There was a courtesan in Mathura named Vasavadatta. Once, she saw a monk named Upagutta, one of Buddha's disciples, a tall and handsome young man who fell desperately in love with him. She sent an invitation to Upagutta, but he replied, "The time has not yet arrived when Upagutta will visit Vasavadatta."

The courtesan was surprised with his reply and sent again for him, saying, "Vasavadatta desires love, not gold, from Upagutta." But, yet again, he made the same enigmatic reply and did not come.

A few months later, Vasavadatta was having a love affair with the chief of the artisans. But, at that time, a wealthy merchant came to Mathura and fell in love with Vasavadatta.

Seeing his wealth and fearing the jealousy of her other lover, she contrived the death of the chief of the artisans and concealed his body under a dunghill.

When the chief of the artisans went missing, his relatives and friends searched for him and found his body.

Then Vasavadatta was tried by a judge, who declared her guilty and condemned to have her ears and nose, hands and feet cut off, and flung into a graveyard.

Vasavadatta had kind to her servants, and one of her maids followed her. Out of love for her former mistress, this maid ministered to her in her agonies and chased away the crows.

Now the time had arrived when Upagutta decided to visit Vasavadatta.

On approaching, Upagutta greeted her kindly, but Vasavadatta said with petulance, "Once this body was fragrant like the lotus, and I offered you my love. In those days, I was covered with pearls and fine muslin. Now I am mangled by the executioner and covered with filth and blood."

Said the young man, "Sister, it is not for my pleasure that I approach you. It is to restore to you a nobler beauty than the charms you have lost. I have seen with my eyes the Buddha, who is walking upon earth and teaching people the doctrine of Dharma. But you would not have listened to the words of righteousness while surrounded with temptations under the spell of passion and desiring worldly pleasures. The charms of a lovely form are treacherous and quickly lead into temptations, which have proved too strong for you. But there is a beauty that will not fade, and if you listen to the doctrine, you will find that peace you have not found in the restless world of pleasures."

Vasavadatta became calm, and spiritual happiness soothed the tortures of her bodily pain. Having taken the threefold refuge, she died in pious submission to the punishment of her crime.

Fifty-Five

THE LUTE STRINGS

On one occasion, when the Blessed One was staying on Vulture Peak Mountain, a monk named Sona was staying near Rajagraha and meditating in seclusion. Although Sona meditated diligently, he was frustrated by his lack of spiritual progress. So he went to the Buddha to ask him why he was not successful in his practice.

The Buddha listened to the monk and said, "Tell me, Sona, in earlier days, when you were a house-dweller, were you not skilled in playing the stringed music of the lute?"

"Yes, Master!" replied Sona.

"And, tell me, Sona, when the strings on the lute were too taut, was your lute tuneful and easily playable?"

"Certainly not, Master."

"And when the strings on the lute were too loose, was then your lute tuneful and easily playable?"

"Certainly not, Master."

"But when, Sona, the strings of your lute were neither too taut nor too loose, and adjusted to an even pitch, did your lute then have a wonderful sound, and then was it easily playable?"

"Certainly, Master."

"Similarly, Sona, if energy is applied too strongly, it will lead to tension. If energy is too slack, it will lead to laziness. Therefore, you should determine the right pitch for your persistence, attune the pitch of the faculties of senses and in this way focus your attention."

Fifty-Six

LUXURIOUS LIVING

While the Buddha was preaching his doctrine in one of the neighborhoods of Sravastti, a man of great wealth came up to him with clasped hands and said, "O Blessed One, pardon me for not saluting you as I ought, but I suffer greatly from obesity, excessive drowsiness, and other complaints, so that I cannot move without pain."

Seeing the luxuries with which the man was surrounded, the Blessed One asked him, "Do you have a desire to know the cause of your ailments?"

When the wealthy man expressed his willingness to learn, the Buddha said, "There are five things which produce the condition of which you complain: opulent dinners, love of sleep, pursuing pleasure, thoughtlessness, and lack of occupation. Exercise self-control at your meals, and take upon yourself some duties that will exercise your abilities and make you useful to your fellowmen. In following this advice you will prolong your life."

The rich man remembered the words of the Buddha and, after some time, having recovered the lightness of his body and youthful buoyancy, returned to the Blessed One. Coming afoot without horses and attendants, he said, "O Master, you have cured my bodily ailments; I come now to seek enlightenment of my mind."

And the Blessed One said, "The foolish men nourish their bodies, but the wise men nourish their minds. He who indulges in the satisfaction of his appetites works his own destruction, but he who walks in the path will have both - the freedom from evil and a prolongation of life."

Fifty-Seven

THE BUDDHA'S FOOTPRINTS

Once when the Blessed One was sitting under a tree, a brahmin astrologer approached him. The astrologer was very puzzled because he saw the footprints of the Buddha on the wet sand and could not believe his eyes. The scriptures that he had been studying for many years taught him about certain signs on the feet of a chakravartin, a man who rules the world. These exact signs the astrologer saw on the wet sand! And he thought, 'Either all the scriptures I have been studying are wrong, or a chakravartin is walking barefoot on this sand.'

Then he followed the footprints in search of this man and found the Buddha sitting under a tree. He was even more puzzled. The face was that of a chakravartin – the grace, the beauty, the power – but the man was a beggar with a begging bowl.

The astrologer touched the feet of the Buddha and asked him, "Who are you? You have puzzled me. You should be a chakravartin, a world ruler. What are you doing here, sitting under this tree? Either all my astrology books are wrong, or I am being delusional, and you are not really here."

The Buddha said, "Your books are absolutely right, but there is something that belongs to no category, not even to the category of a chakravartin. I am nobody in particular."

The astrologer said, "How can you be nobody in particular? You must be a deity who has come to visit the earth!"

The Buddha said, "I am not a deity."

The astrologer said, "Then you must be a gandharva – a celestial musician."

The Buddha said, "I am not a gandharva either."

Then astrologer went on asking, "Then are you a king in disguise?"

And the Buddha responded, "I am a Buddha. I am just awareness and nothing else. I do not belong to any category. Every category is an identification, and I do not have any identity."

Fifty-Eight

THE SOWER

Bharadvaja, a wealthy brahmin farmer, was celebrating his harvest-thanksgiving when the Blessed One came wandering while on his alms round.

Some people paid the Buddha reverence, but the brahmin was angry and said, "O ascetic, it would be more fitting for you to go to work than to beg. Look at me. I plough and sow, and having ploughed and sown, I eat. If you do likewise, you, too, would have something to eat."

The Buddha answered him, "O Brahmin, I, too, plough and sow, and having ploughed and sown, I eat."

"Do you profess to be a farmer?" replied the brahmin. "Where, then, are your bullocks? Where are the seeds and the plough?"

The Blessed One replied, "Faith is the seed I sow: good works are the rain that fertilizes it; wisdom and modesty are the plough; my mind is the guiding-rein; earnestness is the goad I use, and exertion is my draught-ox. This ploughing is ploughed to destroy the weeds of illusion. The harvest it yields is the immortal fruit of liberation."

The brahmin was left highly impressed by the Buddha's words and, having poured rice-milk into a golden bowl, he offered it to the Blessed One.

Fifty-Nine

ON HAPPINESS

Prince Abhaya once asked the Buddha if he had ever said anything that made people feel unhappy. At the time the prince was holding his baby son on his knee.

The Buddha looked at the child and said, "If your son puts a stone in his mouth, what will you do?"

Prince Abhaya replied, "I will get it out straight away even if I have to hurt the child. Because it can be dangerous to the child, and I have compassion for him."

Then the Buddha explained that sometimes out of compassion he said things that people needed to be told but did not like to hear.

Sixty

THE BUDDHA REPLIES TO THE DEVA

On a certain day when the Blessed One dwelt at Jetavana, a celestial deva came to him in the form of a brahmin. The deva asked questions to which the Blessed One responded.

The deva inquired, "What is the sharpest sword? What is the deadliest poison? What is the fiercest fire? What is the darkest night?"

The Blessed One replied, "A word spoken in wrath is the sharpest sword; covetousness is the deadliest poison; passion is the fiercest fire; ignorance is the darkest night."

The deva said, "Who gains the greatest benefit? Who loses most? Which armor is invulnerable? What is the best weapon?"

The Blessed One replied, "He is the greatest gainer who gives generously to others, and he loses most who greedily receives without gratitude. Patience is an invulnerable armor; wisdom is the best weapon."

The deva said, "Who is the most dangerous thief? What is the most precious treasure? Who is most successful in overtaking violence not only on earth but also in heaven? What is the securest treasure-trove?"

The Blessed One replied, "Evil thought is the most dangerous thief; virtue is the most precious treasure. The mind overtakes everything not only on earth, but also in heaven, and immortality is the securest treasure-trove."

The deva said, "What is attractive? What is disgusting? What is the most horrible pain? What is the greatest enjoyment?"

The Blessed One replied, "Good is attractive; evil is disgusting. A bad conscience is the most tormenting pain; deliverance is the height of bliss."

The deva asked, "What causes ruin in the world? What breaks off friendships? What is the most violent fever? Who is the best physician?"

The Blessed One replied, "Ignorance causes the ruin of the world. Envy and selfishness break off friendships. Hatred is the most violent fever, and the Buddha is the best physician."

Then the deva said, "Now I have only one doubt to be solved; please clear it away: What is that fire can neither burn, nor moisture corrode, nor wind crush down, but can reform the whole world?"

The Blessed One replied, "Blessing! Neither fire, nor moisture, nor wind can destroy the blessing of a good deed, and blessings reform the whole world."

Having heard the words of the Blessed One, the deva was full of exceeding joy. Clasping his hands, he bowed down before the Buddha and disappeared.

Sixty-One

ON ENLIGHTENMENT

Once, the Buddha was walking up to the mountain and came across three people: a man sitting and meditating under the tree's shadow, a man sitting and meditating in the sun, and a man dancing away. All three of them were on their path to enlightenment.

When the Buddha passed the first man, the latter asked, "When will I get enlightened?"

The Buddha answered that it would take at least a thousand years for him to get enlightened. The man continued meditating under the tree.

The Buddha then passed the second man who was sitting in the sun. Parts of his skin were badly burnt, but the man continued meditating and stopped only to ask the same question, "How long would it take for me to get enlightened?"

The Buddha told him that it would take at least another thousand years for him to get enlightened. On hearing this, the man thought, 'I have to suffer so much to get enlightened,' and continued meditating in the sun.

As the Buddha passed the third person who was dancing, he heard the same question. Once again the Buddha said, "It will take you another thousand years to get enlightened."

The man had a laugh and continued dancing. At that point in time he got enlightened.

Sixty-Two

LOVING-KINDNESS

While the Buddha was staying at Sravastti, a group of monks, having received subjects of meditation from the Blessed One, proceeded to a forest to spend the rainy season in practice. The arrival of monks disturbed the tree deities inhabiting this forest, and these deities started to harass the monks in diverse ways to scare them away.

As practicing under such conditions was impossible, the monks went to the Buddha and informed him of their difficulties. Thereon the Blessed One instructed the monks in the Metta sutta, a practice in loving-kindness, and advised them to use this sutta for their protection.

The monks went back to the forest and, practicing the instruction conveyed, permeated the whole atmosphere with such radiant thoughts of loving-kindness. The deities became affected by this energy of love and allowed the monks to meditate in peace.

Sixty-Three

ON MERIT

There was a rich man who used to invite all local brahmins to his house and, giving them rich gifts, offered great sacrifices to the gods.

When the Blessed One came to know of this, he said, "If a man each month repeats a thousand sacrifices and gives offerings without ceasing, he is not equal to the one who but for one moment fixes his mind upon righteousness."

The Buddha continued, "There are four kinds of offerings: first, when the gifts are large and the merit is small; secondly, when the gifts are small and the merit is small; thirdly, when the gifts are small and the merit is large; and fourthly, when the gifts are large and the merit is also large.

"The first is the case of the deluded man who takes away life for the purpose of sacrificing to the gods, accompanied by carousing and feasting. Here the gifts are great, but the merit is small indeed.

"Next, the gifts are small and the merit is also small, when from covetousness and an evil heart a man keeps to himself a part of what he intends to offer.

"The merit is great, however, while the gift is small, when a man makes his offering from love and with a desire to grow in wisdom and kindness.

"Lastly, the gift is large and the merit is also large, when a wealthy man, in an unselfish spirit, gives donations and establishes institutions for the best of mankind to enlighten his fellowmen's minds and administer unto their needs."

Sixty-Four

THE BUDDHA'S EXISTENCE

Once King Milinda approached the Buddhist monk named Nagasena and, desiring to know and see the light of knowledge, asked, "O Nagasena, have you ever seen the Buddha?"

"No, indeed."

"But did your teachers see the Buddha?"

"No, indeed."

"O Nagasena, you say you have never seen the Buddha, and you say your teachers did not see the Buddha either. Well, then the Buddha never existed! For there is nothing here to show that he ever did!"

Replied Nagasena, "How do we know that ancient kings, those who were your predecessors in the line of kings, existed?"

"Why doubt? Those kings did exist."

"O King, have you ever seen those ancient kings?"

"No, indeed."

"But did those who instructed you – priests, commanders-in-chief, judges, ministers, – did they see those ancient kings?"

"No, indeed."

"But, O King, if you have never seen those kings of old, and if your instructors did not see those kings either, there is nothing here to show that those kings ever existed!"

"We know that the ancient kings existed by what they have left us. There exists the insignia employed by them: the white parasol, the diadem, the slippers, the yak's tail fan and the jewelled sword. By these, we may know and believe that the ancient kings existed."

"So is it in the case of the Buddha, O King. There is a reason why we may know and believe that the Blessed One existed. What is the reason? There exist the insignia employed by the Buddha: the Four Intent Contemplations, the Four Right Exertions, the Four Bases of Supernatural Power, the Five Sensations, the Five Forces, the Seven Prerequisites of Enlightenment, and the Noble Eightfold Path. By these, we may know and believe that the Blessed One existed."

III

PARABLES

"I have taught the truth which is excellent in the beginning, excellent in the middle, and excellent in the end; it is glorious in its spirit and glorious in its letter. But simple as it is, the people cannot understand it. I must speak to them in their own language. I must adapt my thoughts to their thoughts. They are like children and love to hear tales. Therefore, I will tell them stories to explain the glory of the Dharma." - Gautama Buddha

Sixty-Five

THE BURNING HOUSE

"I will tell you a story," the Buddha said. "Once there was a man of great wealth who had many children. One day, a fire broke out at his place and was burning down the house. The man shouted at his children, who were playing inside the house, to flee. But his children were so absorbed in their games that they had not realized the house was burning down and did not heed the father's warning.

"Then, the wealthy man devised a practical way to lure the children from the burning house. Knowing that the children were fond of interesting playthings, the anxious father called out to them, 'My beloved children, I have some marvellous carts filled with toys here outside the gate for you to play with. Quickly come out of the house and get them!' The wealthy man knew that these things would be irresistible to his children.

"The children eager to play with these new toys rushed out of the house. But instead of the promised carts, the father gave them carts and toys much better than any he had described. The important thing is that the children were saved from the dangers of the house on fire.

"Now I am like that farther. All the living beings are profoundly addicted to tainting pleasures in the world that is just like a burning house full of frightful woes. And even though I teach and command, they neither believe nor accept. So addicted are they to their desires that I have to lure them out of the burning house by promising the marvellous vehicles to them."

Sixty-Six

THE HUNGRY DOG

In one of the regions there was a powerful king who oppressed his people and was hated by his subjects. But when the Buddha came into his kingdom, the king desired much to see him. He went to the place where the Blessed One stayed and asked, "O Monk, can you teach a lesson to the king that will divert his mind and benefit him at the same time?"

And the Blessed One said, "I shall tell you the parable of the hungry dog. Once there was a wicked tyrant. And the god Indra, assuming the shape of a hunter, came down upon earth with the demon Matali, the latter appearing as a dog of enormous size. Hunter and dog entered the palace, and the dog howled so woefully that the royal buildings shook by the sound to their very foundations. The tyrant had the awe-inspiring hunter brought before his throne and inquired after the cause of the terrible bark. The hunter explained that the dog was hungry, whereupon the frightened king ordered to bring the dog food. All the food prepared at the royal banquet disappeared rapidly in the dog's jaws, and still he howled with portentous significance. More food was sent for, and all the royal store-houses were emptied, but in vain. Then the tyrant grew desperate and asked, 'Will nothing satisfy the cravings of that beast?' 'Nothing,' replied the hunter, nothing except perhaps the flesh of all his enemies.' 'And who are his enemies?' anxiously asked the tyrant. The hunter replied, 'The dog will howl as long as there are people hungry in the kingdom, and his enemies are those who practice injustice and oppress the poor.' The oppressor of the people, remembering his evil deeds, was seized with remorse, and for the first time in his life he began to listen to the teachings of righteousness."

Then the Blessed One addressed the king, who had turned pale, and said, "The Buddha can quicken the spiritual ears of the powerful, and when you hear the dog bark, think of the teachings of the Buddha, and you may still learn how to pacify the monster."

Sixty-Seven

THE PATIENT ELEPHANT

While the Blessed One was residing in the Jeta's Grove, there was a householder living in the city of Sravastti known to all his neighbors as patient and kind, but his relatives were wicked and contrived a plot to rob him. One day they came to the householder and with all kinds of threats took away a goodly portion of his property. He did not go to court to complain but tolerated with great forbearance the wrongs he suffered. The neighbors wondered and began to talk about it, and rumors of the affair reached the ears of monks in Jetavana. While the monks discussed the occurrence in the assembly hall, the Blessed One entered and asked, "What was the topic of your conversation?" And they told him.

Said the Blessed One, "The time will come when the wicked relatives will find their punishment. O Monks, this is not the first time that this occurrence took place; it has happened before," and he told them an old tale.

"Once upon a time, when King Brahmadatta ruled at Benares, the Future Buddha was born in the Himalayan region as an elephant. He grew up strong and big and ranged the hills and mountains, the peaks and caves of the torturous woods in the valleys. Once the elephant saw a pleasant

151

tree and took his food, standing under it. Then some impertinent monkeys came down out of the tree and, jumping on the elephant's back, insulted and tormented him greatly; they took hold of his tusks, pulled his tail and disported themselves, causing him much annoyance. The Future Buddha, being full of patience, kindliness and mercy, took no notice of their misconduct which the monkeys repeated again and again.

"One day, the spirit that lived in the tree addressed the elephant, saying, 'Friend, why do you put up with the impudence of these bad monkeys?'

"The Future Buddha, on hearing this, replied, 'If to prevent these monkeys' ill-treatment I start abusing them, how can I proceed on the noble path? How is that a wholesome action? But these monkeys will do the same to others thinking them to be like me. If they do it to any rogue elephant, he will punish them indeed, and I shall be delivered both from their annoyance and the guilt of having done harm to others.'

"A few days after, the Future Buddha went elsewhere, and another elephant, a savage beast, came and stood in his place. The wicked monkeys, thinking he was like the old one, climbed upon his back and did as before. The rogue elephant seized the monkeys with his trunk, threw them upon the ground, and trampled them under his feet."

The Buddha had ended this tale and identified the births, saying, "At that time the mischievous monkeys were the wicked relatives of the good man, the rogue elephant was the one who will punish them, but the virtuous noble elephant was the Buddha himself in a former incarnation."

After this discourse one of the monks rose and asked, "I have heard the doctrine that wrong should be met with wrong and the evil doer should be checked by being made to suffer, for if this were not done, evil would increase and good would disappear. What shall we do?"

Said the Blessed One, "You shall not do evil for evil nor return hate for hate. Neither think that you can destroy wrong by retaliating evil for evil and thus increasing wrong. Leave the wicked to their fate, and their evil deeds will sooner or later in one way or another bring on their punishment."

Then the Buddha uttered this verse:
Who harms the man who does no harm,
Or strikes at him who strikes him not,
Shall soon some punishment incur
Which his own wickedness begot.

Sixty-Eight

RESCUE IN THE DESERT

One of the Buddha's disciples was full of energy and zeal for the truth. But when he was living under a vow to complete a meditation in solitude, he had a moment of weakness. He thought, 'What is the use of a monk's life if I am not able to attain the insight of meditation to which I have devoted myself?' And he left the solitude and returned to the Jetavana Monastery.

When the other monks saw him, they said, "You are making a mistake of taking a vow and then giving up the attempt to carry it out." Then they took him to the Buddha. When the Blessed One saw them, he said, "I see, O Monks, that you have brought this brother here against his will. What has he done?"

"O Master, this brother, having taken the vows of sanctifying a faith, decided to abandon the endeavor to accomplish it."

Then the Buddha asked the monk, "Is it true that you have given up trying?"

"It is true, O Blessed One," the monk replied.

Then the Buddha said, "This present life of yours is a time of grace. If you fail now to reach a peaceful state, you have to suffer remorse in future existences. How is it, brother, that you have proved so irresolute? In former states of existence you were full of determination. By your energy alone the men and bullocks of five hundred wagons obtained water in the sandy desert and were saved. How is it that you give up now?"

By these few words that brother was re-established in his resolution.

Other monks besought the Blessed One, saying, "O Master! Tell us how this was."

"Listen, then!" said the Blessed One, and having thus excited their attention, he told a story.

"Once upon a time, when King Brahmadatta ruled at Benares, the Future Buddha was born in a merchant's family. He grew up and went about trafficking with five hundred carts. One day the Future Buddha arrived at a sandy desert many miles across. The sand in that desert was so fine that when taken in the closed fist, it could not be kept in hand. After the sun had risen, it became very hot so that no man could walk on the sand. Therefore, the merchants took wood, water, oil, and rice in their carts and traveled during the night. And at daybreak they formed a camp, spread an awning over it and passed the day lying in the shade. At sunset they had supper, and when the ground had become cool, they yoked their oxen and went on. The traveling was like a voyage over the sea: a desert-pilot had to be chosen, and he brought the caravan safe to the other side by his knowledge of the stars.

"With only one night left before the men crossed the desert, the caravan set out after supper. The pilot had cushions arranged on the foremost cart, and laying down, he looked at the stars and directed the men where to go. But worn out by lack of rest during the long march, the pilot fell asleep and did not notice that the oxen had turned around and was taking the same

155

road by which they had originally come. The oxen continued for the whole night. Towards dawn the pilot woke up, and observing the stars, he shouted, 'Stop the wagons, stop the wagons!' The day broke just as they stopped, and with the first rays of sunlight the men cried out, 'Why, this is the very encampment we left yesterday! We have no wood left, and our water is all gone! We are lost!'

"Now the Future Buddha said to himself, 'If I lose hope, all these men will perish,' and he walked about while the morning was yet cool. On seeing a tuft of kusa-grass, he thought, 'This could have grown only by soaking up some water beneath it.' And he made men bring a spade and dig in that spot. And they dug sixty cubits deep. And when they had got thus far, the spade of the diggers struck on a rock. As soon as it struck, they all gave up in despair. But the Future Buddha thought, 'There must be water under that rock,' and descending into the well he got upon the stone. Then he applied his ear to it and heard the sound of water gurgling beneath. When he got out, he called his page, 'My lad, if you give up now, we shall all be lost. Do not lose hope. Take this iron hammer, go down into the pit and give the rock a good blow.'

"The lad obeyed and went down full of determination to strike at the stone. The rock split in two and fell below. As it was no longer blocking the stream, the water rose from the bottom to the brim of the well and was equal to the height of a palm tree. And all men drank this water and bathed in it. Then they cooked rice, ate it and fed their oxen with it. And when the sun set, the men put a flag in the well and went to the place appointed. There they sold their merchandise at a good profit and returned to their homes."

After the Blessed One had told the story, he formed the connection, saying, "The page who broke the stone and gave water to the multitude was this brother without perseverance."

Sixty-Nine

THE HAWK

"In the old times, a hawk attacked a quail and caught it. As the hawk was carrying off the quail, the quail lamented, 'I am indeed unfortunate, I possess little merit as I walked in forbidden ground, in a foreign region. If today I had walked in my own ground, in the region of my fathers, this hawk would not have been equal to a combat with me.'

"Asked the hawk, 'Quail, what is your feeding ground? What is the region of your fathers?'

"Replied the quail, 'A field of clods, turned up by the plow.'

"Then the hawk out of confidence and pride, not exerting his strength, not asserting his strength, released the quail, saying, 'Go, quail! Even there you will not escape from me.' Thus the quail went to the field of clods, turned up by the plow. He mounted a big clod and called the hawk, 'Come now, hawk, I dare you!'

"The hawk, again not exerting his strength, not asserting his strength, flapped both his wings and attacked the quail. As the quail knew that the hawk was

157

coming, he entered a crack in that very clod. And, the hawk struck his breast against that very clod."

The Buddha concluded the story, saying, "Thus, O Monks, even animals, when they walk in forbidden ground, fall into the hands of their adversaries; but when they walk in their own ground, in the region of their fathers, they humble their adversaries. Therefore, you also must not walk in forbidden ground, in a foreign region. If you walk in forbidden ground, in a foreign region, Mara will obtain entrance. If you walk in a lawful ground, in the region of the fathers, Mara will not obtain entrance."

Seventy

HOUSEMISTRESS VEDEHIKA

In the old times, in the city of Sravastti lived a housemistress named Vehedika known for her gentleness and tranquility. And this housemistress had a servant named Blackie who was capable and industrious.

Once the following thought occurred to Blackie, 'My lady housemistress has an excellent reputation of being gentle and tranquil. But does she in fact not possess any inward temper or does not reveal her inner temper? It is possible that because I have performed all the duties well, she did not reveal her inward temper. Suppose I were to test her!'

Accordingly, Blackie got up late in the day. And Vedehika asked Blackie, "Why did you get up so late?"

The servant replied, "For no reason at all, my lady."

On hearing this, the housemistress frowned in anger and said, "For no reason at all, worthless servant, you got up so late!"

Then Blackie thought, 'It seems that in fact she possesses an inward temper that she does not reveal. It is solely because I have performed the duties well that she did not reveal an inward temper before. Suppose I were to test her further!'

Accordingly, Blackie got up later in the day. Again Vedehika asked Blackie, "Why did you get up so late?"

The servant replied, "For no reason at all, my lady." And in anger and displeasure the housemistress gave vent to her displeasure in words.

Then Blackie decided to test her housemistress' temper even further. Accordingly, Blackie got up even later in the day.

Again Vedehika asked Blackie, "Why did you get up so late?"

The servant replied, "For no reason at all, my lady." Angered, Vedehika seized the pin of the door-bolt and gave Blackie a blow on the head.

Thereupon the servant, with her head covered in blood, complained to the neighbors, "See the work of the gentle woman! See the work of the meek woman! See the work of the tranquil woman! For this is the way a lady acts who keeps but a single servant." After this Vedehika acquired a reputation of a cruel and evil woman.

Precisely so, a monk may appear ever so gentle, ever so meek, ever so tranquil, so long as unpleasant remarks do not reach him. But when unpleasant remarks reach him, that is the time to find out whether he is in fact gentle, meek and tranquil.

Seventy-One

PRINCE WICKED

Once upon a time, a king named Brahmadatta ruled at Benares. He had a son named Prince Wicked, and Prince Wicked was as tough as a beaten snake. He never spoke to anybody without either reviling him or striking him. The result was that both people inside the palace and outside disliked him. One day, desiring to bathe, Prince Wicked went to the riverbank with a large retinue. At that moment a great cloud arose. The sky became dark.

The prince said to his slaves and servants, "Servants! Take me to the midstream, bathe me and bring me back."

The servants led him but whispered to each other, "This prince is a bird of evil omen. Let's kill this wicked man right here!" So saying, they plunged the prince into the water and returned to the king.

The king asked, "Where is my son?"

The servants replied, "We do not know, your majesty. A raining cloud arose. We returned, supposing that he must have gone ahead of us."

Then the king went to the riverbank and ordered every man to search here and there. Nobody saw the prince in the darkness caused by the rainy cloud. In fact, the prince was swept along by the river. Seeing a certain tree trunk, he clambered on it and terrified traveled along.

At that time, a resident of Benares, a certain treasurer, who had buried forty gold coins by the riverbank, because of his craving for that wealth had been reborn on top of that wealth as a snake. Furthermore, another man, too, had buried thirty gold coins in that very spot and, because of his craving for that wealth had been reborn on the spot as a rat. The water entered their place of abode. They went out by the same path that the water came in, cleft the stream, and saw the tree trunk bestridden by the royal prince. One climbed up on one end, the other on the other, and both lay down right there on top of the tree trunk.

Moreover, on the bank of that very river there was a certain tree, and in it lived a young parrot. That tree, too, with its roots washed by the water, fell on top of the river. The young parrot, unable to fly while it was raining, went and perched on one side of that very tree trunk. Thus did those four travel together, swept along by the river.

Now, at that time the Future Buddha was reborn in the kingdom of Kasi in the brahmin household. When he reached manhood, he retired from the world and became an ascetic. He took up his abode in a leaf-hut at a certain bend in the river. At midnight, as he was walking up and down, he heard the sound of the profound lamentation of that royal prince. The Future Buddha thought, 'It is not fitting that that man should die in sight of an ascetic like me, endowed with friendliness and compassion. I will pull him out of the water and grant him the gift of life.'

Then he calmed the prince's fears, laid hold of that tree trunk by one end, and pulled it. Powerful as an elephant, with a single pull he reached the bank and, lifting the prince in his arms, set him ashore. Seeing the snake, the rat, and the parrot, he picked them up also, carried them to his hermitage, and lighted a fire. 'The animals are weaker,' thought he. So first he warmed the bodies of the animals and later warmed the body of the royal prince. When he brought food, he first gave it to the animals and later offered fruits and other edibles to the prince. Thought the royal prince, 'This false ascetic does not take it into his reckoning that I am a royal prince, but does honor to animals.' And he conceived a grudge against the Future Buddha.

A few days after that, when all four had recovered their strength and vigor, and the river-freshet had ceased, the snake bowed to the ascetic and said, "It is a great service you have done me. I can repay you for your kindness. In such-and-such a place I have buried forty gold coins. When you need money, come to that place and call me out." Then the snake departed. Likewise, the rat addressed the ascetic, "Stand in such-and-such a place and call me out." Then the rat departed. Likewise, the parrot bowed to the ascetic, saying, "I have no money, but if you need self-sown rice, go to such-and-such place of my abode and call me out." Then the parrot departed. But the prince, because it was his custom to betray his friends, thought, 'If you come to me, I'll kill you!' But aloud he said, "When I am established in my kingdom, come and see me; I'll furnish you with anything you need." Then the prince departed. And shortly, the prince became a crowned king.

Thought the Future Buddha, 'I'll put them to the test!'

First, he went to the snake and called it out. At the mere word, the snake came out, bowed to the Future Buddha, saying, "In this place there are forty gold coins; carry them all out and take them with you!"

Replied the Future Buddha, "Let be as it is. If the occasion arises, I'll think about it." So saying, he let the snake go back.

Then he went to the rat, and the rat behaved just as had the snake. Then he went to the parrot and called it out. The parrot also behaved in the same way. 'Now,' thought the Future Buddha, 'I'll test the king!'

He went and passed the night in the king's garden. The following day, having put on beautiful garments, he entered the city on his alms round. At that moment the king, accompanied by a large retinue, was making a circuit of the city. Seeing the Future Buddha even from afar, he thought, 'Here is that false ascetic who comes to live with me! He does not know yet that for the service he has rendered me, I'll straightway have his head cut off!' Then the king said to his servants, "Here's a false ascetic who comes to ask me for something. Without giving that false ascetic a chance to look at me, take him, conduct him out of the city, beat him at every crossroads, and cut off his head in the place of execution!"

Thus king's servants bound the ascetic and started to conduct him to the place of execution, beating him at every crossroads. The Future Buddha, wherever they beat him, uttered the following stanza:

True is this saying of some men of the world:
Driftwood is worth more than some men!

Some local wise men heard these words and asked him, "But, monk, what is the trouble between you and our king? What have you done to him?"

Then the Future Buddha told them the whole story and added, "I alone, by pulling this man out of a mighty flood, have brought this suffering upon myself. I speak as I do because I have not heeded the words of wise men of old!" Hearing this, warriors, brahmins and residents of the city became enraged and slew the king, a betrayer of friends who had not the slightest conception of the virtues, by hitting him with arrows and spears and rocks and clubs.

The Buddha concluded the story by identifying the personages, saying, "O Monks, not only in his present state of existence has Devadatta tried to kill me; in a previous state of existence as well. At that time, the king was Devadatta, the snake was Sariputta, the rat was Moggallana, and the parrot was Ananda."

Seventy-Two

THIRSTY

A man went wandering on a scorching day. As the hours passed, he became quite thirsty and, imagining a mirage of water far away, chased it as if it were real. As luck would have it, his pursuit of the mirage led him right towards a real riverbank gushing with water. However, the man, now more thirsty than ever, merely stood next to the water without taking so much as a single drink.

A bystander noticed him and asked, "You look extremely thirsty, and yet you have been standing here for a minute without taking a drink."

The man replied, "Well, I am really thirsty, but there is too much water in this river for me, and I can not finish it all!"

This man is comparable to someone who is presented with numerous advantages, with many wise teachings, but refuses to take a single one because he can not maintain all of them.

Seventy-Three

THE DESPOT CURED

King Brahmadatta happened to see a beautiful woman, the wife of a merchant. Conceiving a passion for this woman, he ordered a precious jewel secretly to be dropped into the merchant's carriage. The jewel was missed, searched for, and found. The merchant was arrested on the charge of stealing. The king pretended to listen with great attention to the defence and, with seeming regret, ordered the merchant to be executed while his wife was consigned to the royal harem.

Brahmadatta attended the execution in person, for such sights gave him pleasure, but when the doomed man looked with deep compassion at his infamous judge, a flash of the Buddha's wisdom lit up the king's beclouded mind. While the executioner raised the sword for the fatal stroke, Brahmadatta felt the effect in his own mind and saw himself on the block.

"Hold, executioner!" shouted Brahmadatta. "It is the king whom you should slay!"

But it was too late. The executioner had done the bloody deed. The king fell back in a swoon, and when he awoke, a change had come over him. He

166

had ceased to be the cruel despot and henceforth led a life of holiness and righteousness. The people said that the character of the wise man had been impressed into his mind.

O you, who commit murders and robberies! The evil of self-delusion covers your eyes. If you could see things as they are, not as they appear, you would no longer inflict injuries and pain on your own selves.

Seventy-Four

KING PACETANA

In the past, there was a king named Pacetana. Once King Pacetana addressed a chariotmaker, "Friend, six months from now there will be a battle. Can you make me a new pair of wheels?" And chariotmaker agreed.

After six months less six days the chariotmaker had finished one wheel. King Pacetana then addressed the chariotmaker, "Six days from now there will be a battle. Is the new pair of wheels finished?"

The chariotmaker responded, "In the past six months less six days, O King, I have finished one wheel."

King Pacetana asked, "But can you finish a second wheel for me in the next six days?"

The chariotmaker replied, "I can, O King." Then the chariotmaker finished the second wheel over the next six days. He brought the new pair of wheels to King Pacetana and said, "This is the new pair of wheels I have made."

Then the king asked, "What is the difference between the wheel that took six months less six days to complete and the one that took six days to complete? I do not see any difference between them."

Then the chariotmaker rolled the wheel which took six days to finish. It rolled as far as the impetus carried it, and then it wobbled and fell to the ground. But the wheel that took six months less six days to finish rolled as far as the impetus carried it and then stood still as if fixed on an axle.

The king asked, "Why is it in this way?"

The chariotmaker replied, "The wheel that took six days to finish has a rim that is crooked, faulty, and defective; spokes that are crooked, faulty, and defective; and a nave that is crooked, faulty, and defective. For this reason, it rolled as far as the impetus carried it and then it wobbled and fell to the ground. But the wheel that took six months less six days to finish has a rim without crookedness, faults, and defects; it has spokes without crookedness, faults, and defects; and it has a nave that is without crookedness, faults, and defects. For this reason, it roiled as far as the impetus carried it and then stood still as if fixed on an axle."

In the same way, a monk who has not abandoned crookedness, faults, and defects of the body, speech, and mind falls from the Dharma just as the wheel that was finished in six days fell to the ground. And any monk who has abandoned crookedness, faults, and defects of the body, speech, and mind establishes in the Dharma just as the wheel that was finished in six months less six days remained standing.

Seventy-Five

BLIND MEN AND THE ELEPHANT

A number of disciples went to the Buddha and said, "O Master, there are many hermits and scholars living here in Sravastti who indulge in constant disputes. Some are saying that the world is infinite and eternal and others that it is finite and not eternal. Some are saying that the soul dies with the body and others that it lives on forever, and so forth. What would you say concerning them?"

The Buddha answered, "Once upon a time, there was a certain king who called his servant and told him to go and gather together in one place all the men of Sravastti who were born blind and show them an elephant. The servant did as he was told. Then he said to the blind men assembled there, 'Here is an elephant,' and to one man he presented the head of the elephant, to another its ears, to another a tusk, to another the trunk… the foot, back, tail, and tuft of the tail, saying to each one that it was the elephant.

"When the blind men had felt the elephant, the king went to each of them and asked, 'Tell me, what sort of thing is an elephant?'

"Thereupon, the man presented with the head answered that elephant was

170

like a pot. And the man who had observed the ear said it was like a winnowing basket. The man who had been presented with a tusk said it was like ploughshare. The man who knew only the trunk said it was like a grainery;... the foot, a pillar; the back, a mortar; the tail, a pestle, the tuft of the tail, a brush.

"Then they began to quarrel, shouting, 'Yes it is!' 'No, it is not!' 'An elephant is not that!' 'Yes, it is like that!' and so on, till they came to blows over the matter. And the king was delighted with the scene.

"In the same way, these preachers and scholars holding various views are blind and unseeing. In their ignorance they are by nature quarrelsome, wrangling, and disputatious, each maintaining reality as thus and thus."

Then the Buddha rendered this meaning by uttering this verse:
O how they cling and wrangle, some who claim
For preacher and monk the honored name!
For, quarrelling, each to his view they cling.

Seventy-Six

THE MAN BORN BLIND

There was a man born blind, and he said, "I do not believe in the world of light and appearance. There are no colors, bright or somber. There is no sun, no moon, no stars. No one has witnessed these things." His friends tried to tell him otherwise, but he clung to his opinion. "What you say that you see," he objected, "are illusions. If colors existed, I should be able to touch them. They have no substance and are not real. Everything real has weight, but I feel no weight where you see colors."

A physician was called to see the blind man. He mixed four simples, and when he applied them to the cataract of the blind man, the gray film melted, and his eyes acquired the faculty of sight.

The Buddha is the physician, the cataract is the illusion of the thought 'I am,' and the four simples are the four noble truths.

Seventy-Seven

KASSAPA AND THE WARRIOR

On a certain occasion, Payasi the Warrior said to the monk Kassapa, "O Kassapa, I have a belief that there is no life after death, no soul. I have a belief that there are no living beings reborn without the intervention of parents, no fruition, no ripening of good and evil deeds."

Replied Kassapa, "Warrior, I never encountered or heard such a view. For how can a man say such a thing as this?"

"Here, O Kassapa, let me explain. Suppose my men capture a criminal and arraign him before me. And I say to them, 'Well, batter this man – cuticle and skin and flesh and sinews and bones and marrow – and deprive him of life.' And they batter that man. When he is half-dead, I say to them, 'Now then, fling this man down on his back. Perhaps we may see his soul coming out!' They fling that man down on his back. But no! We do not see his soul coming out! Then I say to them, 'Now then, fling this man down bent double; stand him right side up and upside down; beat him with the hand and with a stick; shake him down. Perhaps we may see his soul coming out!' They do so. But no! We do not see his soul coming out!"

Replied Kassapa, "Well then, Warrior, I will compose a parable for you.

"Suppose a certain trumpeter went to a certain village. Having approached it, he stood in the centre of the village, blew the trumpet three times, set the trumpet on the ground, and sat down on one side. Now, the local villagers thought, 'What makes that charming and delightful sound?'

"They decided to ask the trumpet-blower about this, saying, 'Sire, what makes that charming and delightful sound?'

"Replied the trumpeter, 'Friends, it is that trumpet which makes that charming and delightful sound.'

"On hearing this, the villagers flung that trumpet down on its bottom, saying, 'Speak, O trumpet! Speak, O trumpet!' Alas, the trumpet made no sound! They flung that trumpet down; they stood it right side up and upside down; they beat it with the hand and with a stick; they shook it down. But the trumpet made no sound!

"Then that trumpeter thought, 'How foolish these villagers are! How can they hope to hear the sound of the trumpet by seeking otherwise than in the right way?' And with the villagers watching him, he picked up the trumpet, blew the trumpet three times, and walked off with the trumpet.

"Then, the villagers thought, 'Ah! When this trumpet is connected with a human being, and is connected with exertion, and is connected with wind, then this trumpet makes a sound! But when this trumpet is not connected with a human being, or is not connected with exertion, or is not connected with wind, then this trumpet makes no sound!'

"Precisely so, when this body is connected with life, and is connected with heat, and is connected with consciousness, then it stands and sits and lies down; then it sees objects with the eye, and hears sounds with the ear, and

174

smells odors with the nose, and tastes flavors with the tongue, and touches objects with the body, and understands the doctrine with the mind. But when this body is not connected with life, and is not connected with heat, and is not connected with consciousness, then it does not stand, does not sit, does not lie down, then it does not see objects with the eye, and does not hear sounds with the ear, and does not smell odors with the nose, and does not taste flavors with the tongue, and does not touch objects with the body, and does not understand the doctrine with the mind."

But Payasi the Warrior remained unconvinced and again repeated, "O Kassapa, I still believe that there is no life after death, no soul; there are no living beings reborn without the intervention of parents; there is no fruition, no ripening, of good and evil deeds."

Replied Kassapa, "Warrior, you are a short-sighted man, seeking the next world otherwise than in the right way. Renounce this wicked belief! I will compose another parable for you. Even by a parable does many a man of intelligence in this world comprehend the meaning of a statement.

"Suppose, Warrior, a certain district rose in revolt. And two friends decided to go to that district to try to find some spoils. And they went to that country, to some village or other where there was an uproar. There they saw much hemp thrown away. Seeing this, the first friend told the second friend, 'Here is much hemp thrown away. Now, you pack up a load of hemp, and I'll pack up a load of hemp; we'll both carry off a load of hemp.' And they packed up two loads of hemp.

"They both went with their loads of hemp to some village where there was an uproar. There they saw much hempen thread thrown away. Seeing this, the first friend told the second friend, 'The very thing for which we should have wanted hemp! Here is much hempen thread thrown away! Let's throw away your load of hemp, and I'll throw away my load of hemp; we'll both carry off a load of hempen instead.' 'This load of hemp I have carried a long way, and it is well tied together. Let me alone! Decide for yourself!' the second friend responded. The first friend threw away his load of hemp and took a load of hempen thread.

"So they went to some other village where there was an uproar. There they saw many hempen cloths thrown away. Seeing this, the first friend addressed the second friend, 'The very thing for which we should have wanted hemp or hempen thread! Here are many hempen cloths thrown away! Let's throw away your load of hemp, and I'll throw away my load of hempen; we'll both carry off a load of hempen cloths instead.' 'This load of hemp I have carried a long way, and it is well tied together. Let me alone! Decide for yourself!' the second friend responded. The first friend again threw away his load of hempen thread and took a load of hempen cloths.

"So they went to some other village where there was an uproar. There they saw an abundance of flax, linen thread, linen cloths; cotton, cotton thread, cotton cloths; iron; copper; tin; lead; silver; gold thrown away. Seeing this, the first friend addressed the second friend, 'The very thing for which we should have wanted hemp or hempen thread or hempen cloths, or flax or linen thread or linen cloths, or cotton or cotton thread or cotton cloths, or iron or copper or tin or lead or silver! Here is gold in abundance thrown away! Now you throw away your load of hemp, and I'll throw away my load of silver; we'll both carry off a load of gold.' 'This load of hemp I have carried a long way, and it is well tied together. Let me alone! Decide for yourself!' the second friend responded. The first friend threw away his load of silver and took a load of gold.

"Then they approached their own village. The friend who returned with a load of hemp was welcomed neither by mother and father, nor by children and wife, nor by friends and companions. But the friend who returned with a load of gold was welcomed by mother and father, and by children and wife, and by friends and companions.

"Warrior! You are just like the man in the parable who carries a load of hemp. Renounce, Warrior, your wicked belief! Let it not be to your disadvantage and sorrow for a long time to come."

On hearing the quick-witted answers of Kassapa, Payasi the Warrior understood the doctrine and took the threefold refuge.

Seventy-Eight

BOAR AND LION

Once an elder monk got annoyed by a younger monk and pelted him with dung. On hearing this, the Buddha told this story.

In the old times, there was a lion who made his home in a mountain cave in the Himalayan country. Not far off, near a certain lake, lived many boars. One day the lion killed a buffalo and ate its flesh. Then he descended into that lake, drank water, and started to come out again. At that moment a fat boar was feeding near that lake. The lion, seeing the boar, reflected, 'Some other day I'll eat him. But if he sees me, he may not come back again.'

So fearing that the boar might not come back again, the lion started to steal around by one side on coming out of the water. The boar watched him and thought, 'That lion, when he saw me, dared not come up to me. He is fleeing in fear. Now is the time for me to measure strength with that lion!' And with his head lifted, the boar challenged the lion to battle with him.

The lion heard this and replied, "O boar, today there will be no battle between you and me, but in seven days the battle shall take place at this very spot." So saying, he went his way.

The boar, delighted at the thought of battling with a lion, went and told the news to his kinsfolk. Frightened they said, "Now you will cause the destruction of every one of us. Not knowing how slight is your strength, you desire to battle with a lion. The lion will come and kill every one of us."

The boar, now also frightened, asked, "What shall I do now?"

Said the other boars, "Go to the dunghill, wallow in the muck for seven days, and let your body dry off. On the seventh day, having moistened your body with drops of dew, go to the battleground ahead of the lion and, noting the direction of the wind, stand to the windward. The lion, smelling the odor of your body, will give you the victory and depart."

The boar did so. On the seventh day, there he stood! The lion, smelling the odor of his body, and knowing that he was covered with dung, said, "O boar, that was a beautiful strategy you have devised. Had you not covered yourself with dung, I should have killed you on the spot. But as it is, it is quite impossible for me either to crush you with my jaws or to strike you with my paws. I give you the victory." Thus saying, he recited this verse:

You are filthy, you bristle with muck,
With bad smells you reek, boar.
If you wish to fight,
I give you the victory.

Then the lion turned around, drank water in the lake and went back to his mountain cave. The boar returned to his kinsfolk and said, "I conquered the lion!"

On hearing this, the other boars exclaimed, "One of these days the lion will come back again and kill every one of us." So they scampered off to another place.

Seventy-Nine

THE PRODIGAL SON

Once upon a time, there was a householder's son who went away into a distant country, and while the father accumulated immeasurable riches, the son became miserably poor. This son, while searching for food and clothing, happened to come to the country in which his father lived. The father saw him in his wretchedness, for his son was ragged and brutalized by poverty. The father ordered some of his servants to call him. When the son saw the place where he was conducted, he thought, 'I must have evoked the suspicion of a powerful man, and he will throw me into prison.' Full of apprehension, he made his escape before he saw his father.

Then the father sent messengers out after his son, who was caught and brought back in spite of his cries and lamentations. Thereupon the father ordered his servants to deal tenderly with his son, and he appointed a laborer of lower rank and education to employ his son as a helpmate on the estate. And the son was pleased with his new situation. From the windows of his palace the father watched the new worker. When the son proved himself to be honest and industrious, the father promoted him higher and higher.

After some time, the father summoned his son, called together all his servants, and made the secret known to them. Then the poor man was exceedingly glad and full of joy at meeting his father.

Just so, little by little, must the minds of men be trained for higher truths.

Eighty

THE CRUEL CRANE

One tailor, who used to make robes for the monks, often cheated his customers and prided himself on being smarter than other men. Once he entered into an important business transaction with a stranger and was cheated himself suffering a heavy loss.

On hearing this, the Blessed One said, "This is not an isolated incident in the greedy tailor's fate. In his other incarnations he suffered similar losses. By trying to dupe others, he ultimately ruined himself. The same greedy character lived many generations ago as a crane near a pond, and when the dry season set in, he said to the fishes with a bland voice, 'Care you not anxious for your future welfare? There is at present very little water and still less food in this pond. What will you do should the whole pond become dry in this drought?' 'Yes, indeed!' said the fishes, 'What should we do?' Replied the crane, 'I know a fine, large lake, which never becomes dry. Would you not like me to carry you there in my beak?' When the fishes began to distrust the honesty of the crane, he proposed to have one of them sent over to the lake to see it. When a big carp decided to take the risk for the sake of the others, the crane carried him to a beautiful lake and brought him back in safety. Then the fishes gained confidence in the crane. Of course, the crane took them one by one out of the pond and ate them on a tall varana-tree.

"There was also a lobster in the pond. The crane, wanting to eat him too, said, 'I have taken all the fishes away and put them in a fine, large lake. Come along. I shall take you, too!' 'But how will you hold me to carry me along?' asked the lobster. 'I shall take hold of you with my beak,' said the crane. 'You can drop me if you carry me like that. I will not go with you!' replied the lobster. 'Do not fear,' rejoined the crane, 'I shall hold you quite tight all the way.'

"Then the lobster thought, 'If this crane once gets hold of a fish, he will certainly never let him go in a lake! Now, if he really puts me into the lake, it will be splendid; but if he does not, then I will cut his throat and kill him!' So he said to the crane, 'You will not be able to hold me tight enough, but we lobsters have a famous grip. If you let me catch hold of you around the neck with my claws, I shall be glad to go with you.'

"The crane did not see that the lobster was trying to outwit him and agreed. So the lobster caught hold of his neck with his claws as securely as with a pair of blacksmith's pincers and called out, 'Ready, go!' The crane took him, showed him the lake, and then turned off toward the varana-tree. 'My dear uncle!' cried the lobster, "The lake lies that way, but you are taking me this other way.' Answered the crane, 'Am I your dear uncle? You wanted me to understand, I suppose, that I am your slave, who has to lift you up and carry you! Now cast your eye upon that heap of fish-bones at the root of the varana-tree. Just as I have eaten those fish, every one of them, just so will I devour you also!'

"The lobster then exclaimed, 'Ah! Those fishes got eaten through their own stupidity, but I will not let you kill me. On the contrary, it is you that I am going to destroy. For you, in your folly, have not seen that I have outwitted you. We both die together, for I will cut off this head of yours and cast it to the ground!' Thus saying, he gave the crane's neck a pinch with his claws.

"Then gasping and trembling with the fear of death, the crane besought the lobster, saying, 'O, my friend! Indeed I did not intend to eat you. Grant me my life!' 'Very well! Fly down and put me into the lake,' replied the lobster. And the crane turned round and stepped down into the lake to place the lobster on the mud at its edge. Then the lobster cut the crane's neck through and swam away."

The Buddha had finished this discourse, saying, "Not only now was this man outwitted by his own intrigues, but also in other existences."

Eighty-One

THE RAFT

The Buddha explained the proper attitude to take towards the Dharma through the famous parable of the raft.

The Blessed One said, "O Monks, I shall show you how the Dharma is similar to a raft, being for the purpose of crossing over, not for the purpose of grasping. Listen and attend closely to what I shall say.

"Suppose a man is trapped on one side of a river. On this side of the river, there is great danger and uncertainty; on the far side is safety. But there is no bridge spanning the river, and there is no ferry to cross over. What should he do? The man gathers together logs, leaves, and creepers and by his wit fashions a raft from these materials. By lying on the raft and using his hands and feet as paddles, he manages to cross the river from the dangerous side to the side of safety. Now, what would you think if the man, having crossed over the river, were to carry the raft on his back over the land since it had served him so well before?"

The monks replied that it would not be a sensible idea to cling to the raft in such a way.

The Buddha went on, "What would you think if he were to lay the raft down gratefully thinking that this raft had served him well but was no longer of use and could thus be laid down upon the shore?"

The monks replied that this would be the proper attitude.

The Buddha concluded, "O Monks, when you know the Dharma to be similar to a raft, you should abandon even the good states just as the bad states. So it is with my teachings: it is a raft for crossing over with, not for seizing hold of!"

Eighty-Two

THE WIDOW'S MITE

Once a lone widow who was very poor beheld monks holding a religious assembly. Hearing the monks' prayers, the woman was filled with joy and thought, 'While others give precious things, I have nothing to offer these monks.' Then she searched her possessions in vain for something to give and recollected that sometime before she had found in a dung-heap two coppers, so taking these she offered them forthwith as a gift.

The superior of the monks, a saint who could read the hearts of men, disregarding the rich gifts of others and seeing the deep faith dwelling in the heart of this poor widow, said this verse:

The poor coppers of this widow
To all purpose are more worth
Than all the treasures of the oceans
And the wealth of the broad earth.
As an act of pure devotion
She has done a pious deed;
She has attained salvation,
Being free from selfish greed.

This woman has done as much as if a rich man were to give up all his wealth.

Eighty-Three

MONKEY - GARDENERS

This parable was related by the Buddha in a little village in the country of the Kosalas with reference to a spoiled garden of a certain householder.

In the old times, when King Brahmadatta ruled at Benares, a holiday was proclaimed. From the moment they heard the holiday drum, the residents of the entire city went about making holiday preparations. At that time, many monkeys lived in the king's garden. The gardener went to the leader of the monkeys and said, "This garden is of great use even to you. Here you eat flowers and fruits. A holiday has been proclaimed in the city, and I am going away to celebrate. Can you water the young trees in this garden until I come back?" The monkey agreed. So the gardener gave those monkeys wooden water-pots to water the trees and departed. The monkeys took the wooden water-pots and watered the young trees.

Now the leader of the monkeys said to the monkeys, "Monkeys, the water must not be wasted. When you water the young trees, pull them up by the roots, look at the roots, water plentifully the roots that strike deep, but sparingly the roots that do not strike deep. Later on, we shall have a hard time getting water." The monkeys did as they were told.

189

At that time, a certain wise man saw those monkeys working away in the king's garden and said to them, "Monkeys, why are you pulling up by the roots every one of those young trees and watering them plentifully or sparingly?"

The monkeys replied, "That is what the monkey who is our leader told us to do."

When the wise man heard that reply, he thought, 'Alas! Those who are fools, those who lack wisdom, think that they will do good, but harm is the only thing they do!' And he uttered the following stanza:

Never, in the hands of one who knows not what is good,
Does a good undertaking turn out happily.
A man who lacks intelligence spoils what is good,
Like the monkey who worked in the garden.

Thus the wise man criticized the leader of the monkeys and departed from the garden.

Eighty-Four

THE GOLDSMITH

A goldsmith uses tongs and a furnace to melt gold. If he constantly makes the fire too hot, the gold will get too hot. If he constantly sprays too much water on it, the gold will not be hot enough. If he constantly takes it out to examine it, it will never become refined. However, if he does all these things at their suitable time, and he knows the nature of gold, he will have no problem at all molding and refining it. Just like that, any practitioner needs to attend to these three qualities: focus, determination, and composure. If he properly attends to these things at the right time and circumstance, his mind will become brilliant and pure, just like gold.

Eighty-Five

HITTING A MOSQUITO

On one occasion the Buddha went from the city of Sravastti to the kingdom of Magadha, and journeying about from place to place in that kingdom, he arrived at a certain little village. Now that village was inhabited by some foolish men. One day these foolish men assembled and took counsel together, saying, "When we enter the forest and do our work, the mosquitoes eat us up, and because of this our work is interrupted. Let us, everyone, take bows and weapons, go and fight with the mosquitoes, pierce and cut all the mosquitoes, and thus make way with them."

Then they went to the forest with these thoughts in their minds. But instead of piercing mosquitos, they pierced and hit one another. In grief, they returned and laid down within the village square.

It so happened that the Buddha with his group of monks entered that village for alms. Seeing wounded men lying here and there, the Blessed One asked the village inhabitants, "Here are many injured men. What have they done?"

"O Blessed One, these men started out with the thought in their minds to fight with the mosquitoes. But instead of mosquitos, they pierced one another."

Said the Buddha, "Not only in their present state of existence these foolish men ended up hurting themselves; in a previous state of existence, they also were the very men who wanted to hit mosquitos but ended up hitting something very different."

Then he related the story of the past, "In the old times when King Brahma-datta ruled at Benares, the Future Buddha made his living by trading. At that time, in the kingdom of Kasi, in a certain village dwelt many carpenters. One of these carpenters, an older man, was planting a tree in his garden. Suddenly, a mosquito settled on his head and pierced his skin. The carpenter told his son, 'Son, a mosquito is stinging me on the head. Shoo him away!' 'Father, wait a moment! I'll kill him with a single blow!' the son exclaimed. It so happened that the Future Buddha, having reached that village, was sitting in the carpenter's hut. So, the son took his stand immediately behind his father. Thinking of only hitting a mosquito, he raised a big axe aloft, hit his father's head and killed the carpenter on the spot."

Then the Buddha uttered this verse:
Better an enemy with sense,
Than a friend without it,
For with the words, "I'll kill a mosquito!"
A son – both deaf and dumb! – split his father's skull!

Eighty-Six

WEALTHY MAN'S SPIT

In one of the small towns at the time, everyone competed to gain the favor of an extremely wealthy man. Even if he spitted, someone would hurry to honor him by putting out the spit with their foot. However, one villager never got the opportunity even to do that. So one day, he decided that since everyone beat him to stepping on the spit before it reached the ground, he would carefully observe the wealthy man and step on the spit just as it was leaving his mouth. Incredibly pleased with his plan, he followed through with it the next day and ended up kicking the wealthy man right in his face. Greatly angered, the wealthy man yelled, "You must be a lunatic! Why did you just kick me in the mouth?"

The villager replied, "I did it to gain your favor, Sir. When you spit, everyone else rushes to step and put it in the ground, but I am always too late. So, I stepped on it even before it left your mouth. And now that you know my reason, surely you are pleased by what I did."

The man's mistake was that his timing was wildly off. There is a proper time for everything, and if a person wants to force a benefit before the proper time for it has arrived, it will lead to problems.

Eighty-Seven

GOLDEN SWAN

The Buddha told this story as something that took place in one of his previous lifetimes. At that time, he was a simple man with a wife and three daughters. He was always kind to people and was dearly loved by his family. Unfortunately, he died before he could marry his daughters, and this saddened his soul. When he entered the other world, he observed what was happening on earth and saw that his family was almost poverty-stricken.

So he returned to his family as a beautiful golden swan and said to his wife, "I have come to you in this form. Once a month I shall come and leave one of my gold feathers for you to sell. In this way, you will easily be able to meet all your expenses."

So every month he used to come and leave a gold feather.

The wife was pleased, and the daughters were so happy when they saw their father. The swan used to stay for a few minutes and then leave.

One day an idea entered into the wife's mind, 'My husband may not come regularly, or he may change his mind and stop coming, or he may grow old and die. The best thing is for me to catch him and strangle him the next time he comes so that I take away all his feathers.'

The daughters were shocked by this thought and said, "How can you do this kind of thing, Mother?"

The wife answered, "All right, I will not strangle him. But I will take away all his feathers. If he cannot fly anymore, you will care for your father, so no harm will be done."

The daughters pleaded not to proceed with a wicked plan, but the mother would not listen. The next time the bird came, she caught hold of him by the neck and took away all the feathers, one by one.

It was very painful to the swan as he cried and screamed most pitifully, "What are you doing? I have been so kind to you."

When the wife was finished, the bird, suffering immensely, could not fly anymore. Then all of a sudden, all the gold feathers turned into ordinary white feathers: they no longer were made of gold.

The greedy wife felt miserable because of this change and decided to check her secret box where she kept the gold feathers that she had accumulated but had not yet sold. She knew that she still had many of them, enough to meet her family's expenses for at least six months. But as soon as she opened the box, she found that these feathers, too, had turned into ordinary white feathers.

The three daughters, with great love and affection, each day fed the poor swan and showed him tremendous concern. The mother was now helpless; she fell into remorse. 'This happened because of my greed,' she thought, but she still secretly hoped that the swan would grow new gold feathers. Slowly, the swan's feathers grew back again, but this time they were pure white.

There was no point in taking them, and the bird flew away.

Eighty-Eight

TWO MONKS AND A WOMAN

Two celibate monks were travelling from one monastery to another. After a long walk, they came to a river they had to cross. The river was flooded, and there was no way that they would get across without getting wet. One lady was also at the banks of a river, wanting to cross; she was weeping because she was afraid to cross on her own.

The monks decided to cross the river by walking through the relatively shallow part of the river. Since the lady also needed to get to the other bank, the older monk, without much ado, carried her on his shoulders, and soon they reached the other bank, where he set her down. The lady went her way, and the two monks continued their walk in silence. The younger monk was very upset, finding the other monk's act disturbing.

After a few hours, the younger monk couldn't stand what had happened, which kept filling his mind, so he began to berate the other monk, saying, "We are not allowed to look at women, but you carried that woman!"

"Which woman?" replied the older monk.

"The woman you carried on your shoulders across the river!"

The other monk paused and said with a smile, "I put her down when I crossed the river. Why are you still carrying her?"

IV

DISCOURSES

On one occasion the Blessed One was dwelling at Sravastti in Jeta's Grove, Anathapindika's Park. There he gave several discourses, some of which are presented in this chapter.

Eighty-Nine

UNTYING THE KNOTS

The Buddha came to teach his disciples carrying a beautiful silk handkerchief in his hands. Thousands of disciples were surprised to see such an article in the Buddha's hand.

When the Buddha addressed the gathering, he asked, "What do you see?"

They responded that they saw a beautiful silk handkerchief. Then slowly, the Buddha started to put knots on the handkerchief, one after another, until he put five knots.

Then the Blessed One asked whether it was the same handkerchief.

His disciples answered that it was the same handkerchief, yet different, as it was in knots now.

The Buddha continued, "That is what I want you to understand. You are all Buddha but unable to see the fine silken fabric because you are in knots. I am like the same handkerchief but without knots."

Then the Buddha went on to pull the handkerchief from both sides and asked whether the knots would open this way.

His disciples said that this way the knots will tighten and become more difficult to open.

The Blessed One asked, "Why do you then try to open your knots by pulling? You are making it more complicated. If one had to open these knots, what would be needed to be done?"

One monk answered that he would need to come close, observe and try to understand how the knots were formed. If one saw how they were formed, one would be able to undo them.

Then the Buddha said, "Now, O Monks, go and meditate upon your own knots."

Ninety

ON PARENTS

"O Monks, there are two persons that cannot easily be repaid. Who are they? One's mother and father. Even if one were to carry one's mother on one shoulder and one's father on the other shoulder for a life span of a hundred years, one still would not have done enough for one's parents, nor would one have repaid them.

"Even if one were to establish one's parents as the supreme lords and rulers over this great earth abounding in the seven treasures, one still would not have done enough for one's parents, nor would one have repaid them. For what reason? Parents are of great help to their children; they bring them up, feed them, and teach them about the world.

"But if, when one's parents lack faith, one encourages, settles, and establishes the parents in faith; if, when one's parents are immoral, one encourages, settles, and establishes the parents in virtuous behavior; if, when one's parents are miserly, one encourages, settles, and establishes the parents in generosity; if, when one's parents are unwise, one encourages, settles, and establishes the parents in wisdom - in such a way, one has done enough for one's parents and repaid them."

Ninety-One

ON MIND

"O Monks, suppose a misdirected spike of hill rice or barley were pressed by the hand or foot. It is impossible that it would pierce the hand or the foot and draw blood. For what reason? Because the spike is misdirected. So too, it is impossible that a monk with a misdirected mind would pierce ignorance, arouse true knowledge, and achieve liberation. For what reason? Because the mind is misdirected.

"Suppose a well-directed spike of hill rice or barley were pressed by the hand or foot. It is possible that it would pierce the hand or the foot and draw blood. For what reason? Because the spike is well directed. So too, it is possible that a monk with a well-directed mind would pierce ignorance arouse true knowledge, and achieve liberation. For what reason? Because the mind is well directed.

"Here, having encompassed a mentally corrupted person's mind with my own mind, I understand that if this person were to die at this time, he would be deposited in a bad destination. For what reason? Because his mind is corrupted. It is because of mental corruption that after death some beings are reborn in the plane of misery, in a bad destination, in the lower world.

"Here, having encompassed a mentally placid person's mind with my own mind, I understand that if this person were to die at this time, he would be deposited in a good destination. For what reason? Because his mind is placid. It is because of mental placidity that after death some beings are reborn in a good destination, in a heavenly world.

"Suppose there were a pool of water that was cloudy, turbid, and muddy. Then a man with a good sight standing on the bank could not see shells, gravel and pebbles, and shoals of fish swimming. For what reason? Because the water is cloudy. So too, it is impossible for a monk with a cloudy mind to know his own good, the good of others, or to realize a distinction in knowledge and vision worthy of the noble ones. For what reason? Because the mind is cloudy.

"Suppose there were a pool of water that was clear, serene, and limpid. Then a man with a good sight standing on the bank could see shells, gravel and pebbles, and shoals of fish swimming. For what reason? Because the water is limpid. So too, it is possible for a monk with a limpid mind to know his own good, the good of others, and to realize a distinction in knowledge and vision worthy of the noble ones. For what reason? Because the mind is limpid.

"O Monks, just as sandalwood is declared to be the best of trees with respect to malleability and wieldiness, so too, I do not see even one other thing that, when developed and cultivated, is so malleable and wieldy as the mind. I do not see even one other thing that changes so quickly as the mind."

Ninety-Two

ON MIND ACTIVITY

"O Monks, there are these three types of persons found existing in the world. What are these three? One whose mind is like an open sore, one whose mind is like lightning, and one whose mind is like a diamond.

"What is the person whose mind is like an open sore? This is prone to anger and easily exasperated. Even if he is criticized slightly, he will lose his temper and becomes irritated, hostile, and stubborn; he displays irritation, hatred, and bitterness. Just as a festering sore, if struck by a stick or a shard, will hurt even more, so too this person prone to anger will display more irritation, hatred, and bitterness. This person is said to have a mind like an open sore.

"What is the person whose mind is like lightning? This person understands what suffering is, the origin of suffering, the cessation of suffering and the way leading to the cessation of suffering. Just as in the dense darkness of night, a man with good sight can see forms by a flash of lightning, so too this person understands as it really is.

"What is the person whose mind is like a diamond? This person realizes for himself with direct knowledge, in this very life, the taintless liberation of mind, liberation by wisdom, and having entered upon it, dwells in it. Just as there is nothing that a diamond cannot cut, whether gem or stone, so too, with the destruction of the taints, this person realizes for himself the direct knowledge of liberation.

"These, O Monks, are the three types of persons found existing in the world."

Ninety-Three

ON VIEW

"O Monks, for a person of the wrong view, wrong intention, wrong speech, wrong action, wrong livelihood, wrong effort, wrong mindfulness, wrong concentration, wrong knowledge, and wrong liberation, whatever bodily karma, verbal karma, and mental karma he instigates and undertakes in accordance with that view, and whatever his volition, yearning, inclination, they all lead to what is unwished for, undesired, and disagreeable, to harm and suffering. For what reason? Because the view is bad.

"Suppose a seed of neem or bitter gourd were planted in moist soil. Whatever nutrients it would take up from the soil and the water would all lead to its bitter, pungent, and disagreeable flavor. For what reason? Because the seed is bad. So too, for a person of the wrong view, whatever his volition, yearning, or inclination, they all lead to what is unwished for, undesired, disagreeable, to harm and suffering. For what reason? Because the view is bad.

"Suppose a seed of sugar cane or grape were planted in moist soil. Whatever nutrients it would take up from the soil and the water would all lead to its agreeable, sweet, and delectable flavor. For what reason? Because the seed is good. So too, for a person of right view, whatever his volition, yearning, or inclination, they all lead to what is wished for, desired, and agreeable, to well-being and happiness. For what reason? Because the view is good."

Ninety-Four

ON SENSE PLEASURES

"O Monks, happiness is not the result of gratifying sense desires. Sense pleasures give the illusion of happiness, but in fact they are sources of suffering.

"It is like a leper who is forced to live alone in the forest. His flesh is wracked by terrible pain day and night. So he digs a pit and makes a fierce fire, and he stands over it to seek temporary relief from his pain by toasting his limbs over the fire. It is the only way he can feel any comfort. But, miraculously, after a few years, his disease goes into remission, and he is able to return to normal life in the village. One day he enters the forest and sees a group of lepers toasting their limbs over hot flames just as he once did. He is filled with pity for them, for he knows that in his healthy state he could never bear to hold his limbs over such fierce flames. If someone tried to drag him over the fire, he would resist with all his might. He understands that what he once took to be a comfort is actually a source of pain to one who is healthy."

The Buddha continued, "Sense pleasures are like a pit of fire. They bring happiness only to those who are ill. A healthy person shuns the flames of sense desires."

Ninety-Five

FOUR TYPES OF HORSES

One man decided to ask the Buddha a question about motivation. The Buddha kept silence and then uttered this stance:

There are four horses.
The excellent horse moves before the whip touches its back.
The good horse runs at the lightest touch.
The poor horse does not move till it feels pain.
And then there is the very bad horse.
It stays still until the whip penetrates its marrow.

Then he explained further, "In the running of our lives, men are like these horses. Some of us know that they are the reflection of our own self before any prompting. They know that they are destined to be pure and great, good and whole. They need no goad to change as they are already running towards the light."

Ninety-Six

ON ESSENCE

"All things, O Monks, are made of one essence, yet things are different according to the forms which they assume under different impressions. As they form themselves so they act, and as they act so they are. It is as if a potter made different vessels out of the same clay. Some of these pots are to contain sugar, others rice, others curds and milk; others still are vessels of impurity. There is no diversity in the clay used; the diversity of the pots is only due to the moulding hands of the potter who shapes them for various uses.

"And as all things originate from one essence, they are developing according to one law, and they are destined to one aim: liberation. This liberation comes to you when you understand thoroughly and live according to your understanding that all things are of one essence and there is only one law.

"And the enlightened person is the same to all beings, differing in his attitude only in so far as all beings are different. He has the same sentiments for the high as for the low, for the wise as for the ignorant, for the noble-minded as for the immoral. The great cloud full of rain comes up in this wide universe covering all countries and oceans to pour down its rain everywhere, over all grasses, shrubs, herbs, trees of various species, families of plants of different names growing on the earth, on the hills, on the mountains, or in the valleys. Then the grasses, shrubs, herbs, and wild trees suck the water emitted from that great cloud that is all of one essence and has been abundantly poured down. According to their nature, they will acquire a proportionate development, shooting up and producing blossoms and their fruits in season. Rooted in the same soil, all those families of plants are quickened by the water of the same essence.

"The enlightened person is the same to all, yet knowing the requirements of every being, he does not reveal himself to all alike. He does not impart to them at once the fullness of omniscience but pays attention to the disposition of various beings."

Ninety-Seven

ON POSSESSIONS

One disciple asked the Blessed One, "How to understand the fulfillment of the commandment of giving up property? One student left all things, but the Blessed One continued to blame him for ownership. The other remained surrounded by things but did not deserve the rebuke."

"Ownership is measured not by things but by thoughts. You can have things and not be the owner," the Buddha responded.

The Blessed One constantly advised his disciples to have as few things as possible and not to give material possessions too much time.

Ninety-Eight

ON IGNORANCE

Once the Buddha was seated with his monks in the shade of beautiful sala trees. He picked up a small piece of earth, held it between his thumb and forefinger, and asked, "O Monks, if we compare this piece of earth with Gayasisa mountain, which is larger?"

"Certainly, Gayasisa is much larger, O Master."

"It is like that. For those who have arrived at understanding thanks to their study and practice of the Dharma, their suffering is almost nothing compared with the suffering of those who are submerged in ignorance. Ignorance magnifies suffering by millions of times.

"Suppose someone is struck by an arrow. He will feel pain. But if a second arrow strikes him at the same spot, the pain will be much more than just doubled. And if a third arrow strikes him at that same spot again, the pain will be a thousand times more intense. O Monks, ignorance is the second and the third arrow. It intensifies the pain.

"By virtue of understanding, a practitioner can prevent the pain in himself and others from being intensified. When an unpleasant feeling, physical or mental, arises in him, the wise man does not worry, complain, weep, pound his chest, pull his hair, torture his body and mind, or faint. He calmly observes his feeling and is aware that it is only a feeling. He knows that he is not the feeling, and he is not caught by the feeling. Therefore, the pain cannot bind him. When he has a painful physical feeling, he knows that there is a painful physical feeling. He does not lose his calmness, does not worry, does not fear, and does not complain. Thus the feeling remains a painful physical feeling, and it is not able to grow and ravage his whole being."

Ninety-Nine

THE POISONED ARROW

Once monk Malunkyaputta asked the Buddha, "If the Blessed One knows whether the world is eternal, whether the world is finite, whether the life principle and the body are the same, whether an enlightened person continues to exist after death, please teach me about these things."

The Buddha answered, "Malunkyaputta, I never said 'Follow me, and I will answer your questions!' nor did you say 'I will follow the Blessed One because he will explain these matters!' You are like a person shot with a poisoned arrow who says, 'I will not have this arrow removed until I know who shot it, his name, his family, whether he is tall or short, young or old and so on and so forth…' If this person were to attend to these questions before pulling out the poisonous arrow, he would probably die.

"Malunkyaputta, the religious life does not depend on dogma. Whether the world is eternal or not, whether the world is finite or not, whether the life principle and the body are or are not the same, and whether or not an enlightened person continues to exist after death, there undoubtedly do exist sorrow, discontent, grief and despair, the overcoming of which I teach."

One Hundred

ON COMPETENCE

~ ⚜ ~

"Suppose, O Monks, there existed a mountain-dwelling cow that was foolish, incompetent, inexperienced, and unskilled in walking on rough mountains. It might occur to her, 'I should go to a region where I have never gone before and eat grass that I have never eaten before.' She would set down a front foot and, while it is not yet firmly planted, lift up a hindfoot. She would not go to a region where she had never gone before and eat grass that she had never eaten before, and she would not return safely to the region where she was staying before. For what reason? Because that mountain-dwelling cow was foolish, incompetent, inexperienced, and unskilled in walking on rough mountains.

"So too, some monk who is foolish, incompetent, inexperienced, and un-skilled, when, secluded from sensual pleasures, secluded from unwholesome states, he enters and dwells in the first jhana, which consists of rapture and pleasure born of seclusion, accompanied by thought and examination. He does not pursue that object, does not develop it, cultivate it and does not focus on it well. It occurs to him, 'With the subsiding of thought and examination, I should enter and dwell in the second jhana.' But he cannot enter and dwell in the second jhana. Then it occurs to him, 'Secluded from sensual pleasures, secluded from unwholesome states, I should return and dwell in the first jhana.' However, now he cannot return and dwell in the first jhana either. This is called a monk who has dropped away from both fallen away from both. He is just like that mountain-dwelling cow that was foolish, incompetent, inexperienced, and unskilled in walking on rough mountains.

"Suppose there existed a mountain-dwelling cow that was wise, competent, experienced, and skilled in walking on rough mountains. It might occur to her, 'I should go to a region where I have never gone before and eat grass that I have never eaten before.' When setting down a front foot, she would firmly plant it and only then lift up a hindfoot. She would go to a region where she had never gone before and eat grass that she had never eaten before, and she would return safely to the region where she was staying before. For what reason? Because that mountain-dwelling cow was wise, competent, experienced, and skilled in walking on rough mountains.

"So too, some monk who is wise, competent, experienced, and skilled, when, secluded from sensual pleasures, secluded from unwholesome states, he enters and dwells in the first jhana, which consists of rapture and pleasure born of seclusion, accompanied by thought and examination. He pursues that object, develops it, cultivates it and focuses on it well. It occurs to him, 'With the subsiding of thought and examination, I should enter and dwell in the second jhana.' Now he can enter and dwell in the second jhana, as well as he can return safely and dwell in the first jhana. This is called a monk who has achieved both states. He is just like that mountain-dwelling cow that was wise, competent, experienced, and skilled in walking on rough mountains."

One Hundred and One

ON TEACHINGS

"O Monks, there are various kinds of assemblies: assemblies of nobles, of brahmins, of householders, of monks, and of other beings. When I enter any assembly, I always speak in the audience's voice. I speak to them in their language and with a discourse instruct and inspire them.

"I teach a doctrine that is like the ocean, having the same eight wonderful qualities. Both the ocean and my doctrine become gradually deeper. Both preserve their identity under all changes. Both cast out dead things upon the dry land. As the great rivers, when falling into the main, lose their names and are reckoned as the great ocean, so all the castes, having renounced their lineage and entered the Sangha, become monks. As the ocean is the goal of all streams and of the rain from the clouds, so my doctrine is the goal for all beings. As the great ocean has only one taste, the taste of salt, so my doctrine has only one flavor, the flavor of liberation. Both the ocean and my doctrine are full of gems, pearls and jewels. Both the ocean and my doctrine afford a dwelling-place for mighty beings.

"Dharma is pure and does not discriminate between rich and poor. This doctrine is like water which cleanses all without distinction. This doctrine is like fire which consumes all things that exist between heaven and earth, great and small. This doctrine is like unto the heavens, for there is ample room in it for the reception of all."

One Hundred and Two

ON FRIENDSHIP

One time Ananda approached the Buddha, paid homage, and said, "O Master, good friendship, good companionship, good comradeship is half of the holy life!"

Replied the Buddha, "Not so, Ananda! Good friendship, good companionship, good comradeship is the entire holy life. When a monk has a good friend, a good companion, a good comrade, it is to be expected that he will develop on the noble path."

One Hundred and Three

ON DIRECTION

"O Monks, there are these four types of persons found existing in the world. What are these four? The one heading from darkness to darkness, the one heading from darkness to light, the one heading from light to darkness, and the one heading from light to light.

"How is a person heading from darkness to darkness? This person has been reborn in a low family, one that is poor, with little food and drink, that subsists with difficulty; and he is unsightly and with much illness. And he engages in misconduct by body, speech, and mind. In consequence, after death he is reborn in the plane of misery, in a bad destination. It is in this way that a person is heading from darkness to darkness.

"How is a person heading from darkness to light? This person has been reborn in a low family, one that is poor, with little food and drink, that subsists with difficulty; and he is unsightly and with much illness. Yet he engages in good conduct by body, speech, and mind. In consequence, after death he is reborn in the plane of happiness, in a good destination. It is in this way that a person is heading from darkness to light.

"How is a person heading from light to darkness? This person has been reborn in a high affluent family, one that is rich, with great wealth and property; and he is handsome, attractive, graceful. Yet he engages in misconduct by body, speech, and mind. In consequence, after death he is reborn in the plane of misery, in a bad destination. It is in this way that a person is heading from light to darkness.

"How is a person heading from light to light? This person has been reborn in a high affluent family, one that is rich, with great wealth and property; and he is handsome, attractive, graceful. And he engages in good conduct by body, speech, and mind. In consequence, after death he is reborn in the plane of happiness, in a good destination. It is in this way that a person is heading from light to light.

"These are the four types of persons found existing in the world."

One Hundred and Four

ON VIOLENCE

One disciple asked the Buddha, "If somebody hits me, what am I supposed to do?"

The Buddha said, "Suppose you are walking and a tree branch of a tree falls and hits you. What are you going to do?"

The disciple responded, "What can I do? It was just an accident, a mere coincidence that I was under the tree and the branch fell down."

The Buddha said, "Just like that! When somebody being mad and angry hits you, it is like a branch falling on you. Don't be disturbed by this, don't be distracted by this. Just keep on following your ways as if nothing has happened."

ON CLOUDS

"O Monks, there are these four types of clouds. What are these four? The one that thunders but does not rain; the one that rains but does not thunder; the one that neither thunders nor rains; and the one that both thunders and rains. These are the four types of clouds. So too, there are four types of persons similar to clouds found existing in the world.

"How is a person who thunders but does not rain? This is a person who is a talker, but not a doer. It is in this way that a person is one who thunders, but does not rain.

"How is a person who rains but does not thunder? This is a person who is a doer, but not a talker. It is in this way that a person is one who rains, but does not thunder.

"How is a person one who neither thunders nor rains? This is a person who is neither a talker, nor a doer. It is in this way that a person is one who neither thunders, nor rains.

"How is a person one who both thunders and rains? This is a person who is both a talker and a doer. It is in this way that a person is one who both thunders and rains.

"These are the four types of persons similar to clouds found existing in the world ."

One Hundred and Six

ON DEPENDENCIES

Once Ananda approached the Blessed One, paid homage to him, and said, "O Master, what is the purpose and benefit of wholesome virtuous behavior?"

The Blessed One replied, "Ananda, the purpose and benefit of wholesome virtuous behavior is non-regret."

"And what is the purpose and benefit of non-regret?"

The Blessed One replied, "The purpose and benefit of non-regret is joy."

"And what is the purpose and benefit of joy?"

"The purpose and benefit of joy is rapture."

"And what is the purpose and benefit of rapture?"

"The purpose and benefit of rapture is tranquility."

"And what is the purpose and benefit of tranquility?"

"The purpose and benefit of tranquility is pleasure."

"And what is the purpose and benefit of pleasure?"

"The purpose and benefit of pleasure is concentration."

"And what is the purpose and benefit of concentration?"

"The purpose and benefit of concentration is the knowledge and vision of things as they really are."

"And what is the purpose and benefit of the knowledge and vision of things as they really are?

"The purpose and benefit of the knowledge and vision of things as they really are is disenchantment."

"And what is the purpose and benefit of disenchantment?"

"The purpose and benefit of disenchantment is dispassion."

"And what is the purpose and benefit of dispassion?"

The Blessed One replied, "The purpose and benefit of dispassion is knowledge and liberation. Thus, Ananda, wholesome virtuous behavior progressively leads to the foremost."

One Hundred and Seven

ON KARMA

"Suppose, O Monks, a man drops a lump of salt into a small bowl of water. Would that lump of salt make the small quantity of water in the bow salty and undrinkable?"

"Yes, Master. Because the water in the bowl is limited, thus that lump of salt would make it salty and undrinkable."

"Suppose a man drops a lump of salt into the river Ganges. Would that lump of salt make the river Ganges salty and undrinkable?"

"No, Master. Because the river Ganges contains a large volume of water, thus that lump of salt would not make it salty and undrinkable."

"Suppose, some person has created trifling bad karma and it leads him to hell, while some other person has created exactly the same trifling bad karma, and it is to be experienced slightly in this very life without even a slight residue. What kind of person creates trifling bad karma that leads him to hell? A person who is undeveloped in body, virtuous behavior, mind, and wisdom. What kind of person creates exactly the same trifling bad karma, and yet it is to be experienced slightly in this very life without even a slight residue? A person who is developed in body, virtuous behavior, mind, and wisdom."

One Hundred and Eight

ON CHARACTERISTICS

"Whether Buddhas arise, O Monks, or whether Buddhas do not arise, there are three facts. It remains a fact and a necessary constitution of being that all conformations are transitory. It remains a fact and a necessary constitution of being that all conformations are suffering. It remains a fact and a necessary constitution of being that all conformations are lacking a self. Any Buddha discovers and masters these facts, and when he has discovered and mastered them, he announces, proclaims, minutely explains them."

On hearing this, one disciple, who still had some doubt left in his heart, asked the Blessed One, "The Buddha teaches that all conformations are transient, that all conformations are subject to suffering, that all conformations are lacking a self. How then can there be liberation, a state of eternal bliss?"

And the Blessed One answered, "There is, O Monks, a state where there is neither earth, nor water, nor heat, nor air; neither infinity of space nor infinity of consciousness, nor nothingness, nor perception nor non-perception; neither this world nor that world; neither sun nor moon. It is the uncreate. It is neither coming nor going nor standing; neither death nor birth. It is without stability and without change. It is the eternal, which

234

never originates and never passes away. There is an unborn, unoriginated, uncreated, unformed. Since there is an unborn, unoriginated, uncreated and unformed, there is an escape from the born, originated, created, formed."

SOURCES

Articles on Buddhist Parables and Similes, Mrs. C. A. F. Rhys Davids, Journal of the Pāli Text Society for 1906-1908.

Buddhaghosha's parables, translated from Burmese by Captain F. Rogers and Müller, F. Max, Trubner & Co, 1870
Buddhist Parables, translated from Pali by Eugene Watson Burlingame, 1922

Great Disciples of the Buddha: Their Lives, Their Works, Their Legacy, Nyanaponika Thera and Hellmuth Hecker, Wisdom Publications, 2003

Hari Om Tat Sat. The Divine Sound: That is the Truth. Osho. Rebel Pub. House, 1989

Manoratha Purani, Buddhaghosa's Commentary on the Anguttara Nikaya, Mabel Bode, The Journal of the Royal Asiatic Society, 1893

Numerical Discourses of Buddha, translated by Anguttara Nikaya, Bhikku Bodhi. Wisdom Publications, 2012

Samyutta Nikaya Sutra, An Anthology, M. O'C. Walshe, Wisdom Publications, 2003

The Buddhacaeita, Acts of the Buddha, E.H.Johnston, D.Litf. Baptist Mission Press, 1936

The Gospel Of Buddha, Paul Carus, The Open Court Publishing Co, 1894

The Jataka; or, Stories of the Buddha's Former Births, edited by E. B. Cowell, vol. 1 and vol. 2, Cambridge University Press, 1895

The Katha Sarit Sagara Or Ocean of the Streams of Story, translated from Sanskrit by C. H. Tawney, Baptist Mission Press, 1880

29642092R00146